Half-Baked Love

Half-Baked Love

Navigating the Messy Middle of Divorce

VERONICA COLÓN

Half-Baked Love
Copyright ©2022 Veronica Colón

Published by Veronica Colón LLC

All rights reserved. No portion of this book may be reproduced, stored in a retrieval system, or transmitted in any form or by any means—electronic, mechanical, photocopy, recording, scanning, or other—except for brief quotations in critical reviews or articles, without the prior written permission of the author or publisher.

ISBN: 978-0-578-28776-8 (paperback)
ISBN: 978-0-578-38793-2 (hardcover)
ISBN: 978-0-578-38794-9 (e-book)

Edited by Ronei L. Harden-Moroney, www.roneiharden.com

Author Photos by Kaitlin Pointer, www.kaitlinpointer.com

Book Design by James Woosley, FreeAgentPress.com

For Nava

This book's for you, baby girl!

This was my biggest dream my whole life and it finally happened—not what I thought I would write about it, but that's not the point.

I want you to chase your dreams and really make them happen regardless of how hard and painful life gets.

I wanted to lead by example and show you hard things can be done.

That pain can be the catalyst to purpose.

You are my driving force and I absolutely adore you.

I'm so thankful God let me be your mama, Nava.

I love you so much.

CONTENTS

Chapter 1: Wretched Flesh 1

Chapter 2: I'm Fine, Really 15

Chapter 3: It Is Well, Dear Soul 35

Chapter 4: To Divorce or Not? 49

Chapter 5: The Sorry You'll Never Get.......................... 65

Chapter 6: A Change of Heart.. 77

Chapter 7: Love Again 91

Chapter 8: A Hug A Day 107

Chapter 9: Filing Day... 121

Chapter 10: Half-Baked Love...................................... 135

Acknowledgements 157

About the Author 161

CHAPTER 1

Wretched Flesh

I DIDN'T DECIDE ONE DAY to wake up so bitter. It caught me by surprise—not because I felt this way, but because it was all-consuming. I was casually scrolling through Instagram one day (everyone's favorite escape) when it hit me out of nowhere. Man, I am so angry! Like FURIOUS—maybe too furious. I feel justified in my anger, secure that anyone in my present circumstances wouldn't hold it against me. But it felt like TOO MUCH.

There was a time in my life when I would allow myself to feel such anger. However, that girl was long gone and, in her place, stood me—a woman carrying around shattered pieces of her heart, desperately trying to hold it together. My life is on replay in my head, wishing it had the soundtrack to *The Greatest Showman*. No one tells you about this level of pain and agony. Here I thought I had already survived my worst days.

This story begins where I am right now—hurt and afraid. Afraid of the million what-ifs in my head. Though none of them seem that scary, in and of themselves, they seem so ***intense***. Fear is making me angry. I never considered myself to be a person who struggles with fear. Most days, I feel incredibly courageous. A silent pep-talk, when I'm feeling less than one hundred percent, usually keeps things rolling. But lately, I can't. I've reached the point where if I don't surrender this or deal with it, I will drown in it.

I'm still technically considered a newlywed, but my marriage is far from a fairy tale romance. In fact, it's more like a horror story. Our marriage barely passed the six-month mark when I discovered my husband was having an affair. I was also pregnant with our first child. Perhaps the cruelest dose of reality ever dealt to me. It did not prepare me for this life, and many days, I denied it was mine at all.

I threw myself into motherhood because my daughter was all I had. Well, her and Jesus. How was I supposed to fix my shattered heart? The interesting thing for me is that it wasn't so much the affair, but everything that happened before, during, and after. You analyze every moment and punish yourself for not seeing it sooner. You blame yourself for either making the wrong choice or for being so naïve. I don't blame myself for the affair. My husband's brokenness is not my fault, and I will not own his own mistakes. I have enough on my plate to go around for someone else's sloppy seconds. Truthfully, I've taken way too many marriage courses and read too many books to accept an affair as being my fault. Could I have done things differently? Of course, but in my situation, I never had the opportunity to correct what was wrong. He cheated on me and explained it later.

My daughter was born four short weeks after my husband confessed. When I say that I felt like it ripped my heart out of my chest, those words don't adequately describe my emotions. What I saw before me was not only a man who deeply hurt me for no reason other than selfishness and immaturity, but also a severely fractured person. Compassion fell upon me. I saw before me the shell of the man my husband used to be, his entire humanity broken before me, and my heart hurt more for his pain than mine. At that moment, I realized the design of marriage was for holiness in ways I couldn't understand.

Marriage - A Holy Covenant

Right now, you're probably thinking, "What?! You felt compassion for him? Why? He's a jerk!" and every expletive you want to insert. He is all those things and more, I'm sure, but he's also a very damaged human being. When you research and study the history and core of human psychology, you discover different factors that motivate behavior. Much of human behavior finds its roots in selfishness and fear. God's design for marriage is a direct representation of His relationship with us. Husbands are to love their wife as Christ loves the church. How much did He love the church? He died for her and gave Himself up for her. God loves His Church. He honors her, cherishes her, and makes good plans for her (Ephesians 5:25-33). He doesn't destroy, abuse, neglect, or break her.

Whether you're a Christian or not, these are still great principles to live by. A marriage is supposed to be united by more than a piece of paper. It's hard when one person takes it seriously and the other one doesn't; when one person will go the distance and keep putting in the effort to love more and the other one doesn't. And it is especially annoying when the person putting in the least amount of effort is the one who has caused the greatest offense. But that makes perfect sense, doesn't it? The person who is struggling the most to love themselves is the person doing the damage. Hurting people hurt people.

I remember once, before my ex and I married, sitting at dinner with some dear friends of ours that were visiting from Australia and she uttered the words, ". . . marriage and children are for holiness." She and her husband have been married for decades and I figured she must know what she's talking about. Yet still, what a funny thing to say!

I didn't understand it at the time and truthfully it took several years before the revelation of those words were fully known. If I'm being honest, I thought my vows had ended because of the affair. I didn't continue to show up the same anymore. I was not available for the "holiness" in this—translation, the sacrifice. Love had left the building because I was wronged. I didn't want to love or honor or forgive. Yet, that is exactly when its needed. You GROW into marriage; you die to yourself (holiness) and your own need to be right. There's a scripture that fascinates me:

> **"Let love and faithfulness never leave you:**
> **bind them around your neck,**
> **write them on the tablet of your heart."**
>
> — Proverbs 3:3-4

I erased the idea of love—I did not want it to bear all things or cover a multitude of sins (1 Peter 4:8). Hindsight is always 20/20, right?

Marriage and children will test every selfish thing in you. They will test your patience, your compassion, your love, your self-control, and your gentleness—refining all the fruits of the Spirit. You will be tested but ultimately you decide if you grow into the muchness of marriage. It's pass or fail daily, but don't worry—you can keep trying.

Can you relate? Think about your daily life and how many times we test those areas in marriage—in any relationship, really. If you are breathing, you are bumping up against one of your fruits, but nothing highlights them more than marriage and children. Thankfully, our babies are a lot cuter than our husbands and, because you are the mom, it's not as hard for you to surrender and win in these areas as it is with your husband or the person who hurt you.

I Don't Like You Right Now

In the case of my jerk-face husband, I don't like him very much right now. I mean, rightfully so, but I still love him because love is a choice, right? There are so many moments that stand out in my mind, one being me sobbing in my bathroom, with the lights off, nine months pregnant. My body was shaking from the intensity of all my emotions. I had only felt emotions this intense two other times—one being when my dog died unexpectedly and the other when at twenty weeks pregnant, they couldn't find my daughter's heartbeat. Both involving death, or potential death. There I was, bawling my eyes and heart out because something died. The expectation of who I thought my husband was had died. My idea of marriage died. My heart died. I died.

Unfortunately, I know more women who can relate to this scenario, perhaps not in its exact details, but the emotions are the same. Grief and death are such all-consuming feelings. Your body cries out to escape from it. Your flesh screams for relief. You hold yourself at night to fall asleep on your tear-soaked pillow, wondering if it will ever not hurt this much again. You wake up the next day in a fog of pain, wishing that it was all a horrible nightmare. It's not. This is our life and we are going to get through this.

I was a new wife and mother, but I felt like he stripped away the title of wife from me. A giant "Just kidding!" sign hanging over my head. Thought you were going to live happily ever after? Just kidding! Honestly, I don't know what I thought marriage would look like; I just knew it wasn't supposed to look/feel like this. I did the only responsible thing—throw all my energy into taking care of my newborn child. Mind you, motherhood gave me no choice, as my child had colic and was a very light sleeper. It tested every facet of my being. I was dying to my wretched flesh.

My daughter was and is a dazzling light at the end of a very long and dark tunnel. God gave her to me as a gift of joy in my life. She has been my driving force to seek healing and freedom from this pain I carry. Being a mother has also revealed the areas of selfishness in my heart and areas where I need to achieve balance. Let's be honest—there is no guilt like mom guilt. It puts two of the most important areas of my life to the test daily, and most days, I feel like I'm failing.

Am I really failing, though? I mean, my daughter is alive and well. I'm alive. Heck, I even showered and brushed my teeth today. That is a WIN! Listen, if you've never been in this situation, you won't get it. Being a first-time mom while dealing with a shitty marriage is LIFE ALTERING! Your brain is in straight survival mode and sometimes showering isn't survival; sleep is. Brushing your teeth isn't survival; drinking some coffee before the baby wakes up is. Before I gave birth to my daughter, I read this quote. I still have it on my phone because it resonates with me:

> *"To be a good mother while my heart was breaking was one of the hardest roles I've ever had to play."*
> — Unknown

I promise you—life is not supposed to be this way. Everything inside me is screaming to make this stop. My heart is being pulled in two polar directions. One says, "F#ck him, he's an idiot, he ruined your life, you don't deserve this," etc. All things that are true. The other part of my heart says, "He's only human, Veronica." He messed up badly, but it's not impossible to reconcile this. Hard, maybe, but not impossible. I am at war. My heart is at war with itself and sometimes my body responds to that inner struggle with raging anger, an ocean of tears, and no sleep.

It's normal though, right? After all, what normal person wouldn't have this rollercoaster of emotions every day? The hardest thing to navigate is this tension within me. It's the wanting to fight for my marriage and see justice and then, equally, wanting to walk away from it. Up to this point in my life, I've navigated my trauma on my own. The people who have caused that trauma were, in no way, shape, or form, invited to continue in my life. I eliminated them. But this is marriage, so what do I do now? For some people, this doesn't even weigh on their minds, but it plagues me.

When I said I do, I meant it. I meant it with every fiber of my being. I did not know it was going to turn out like this. But I still mean it. I do. I DO! I do pick you, even though you have completely betrayed my trust and shattered my heart into a billion pieces. Your selfishness has ruined my idea of a happy pregnancy, a peaceful transition to birth, motherhood, parenthood, and marriage. All of it ruined, and I can have none of that back. That grief alone inundates me.

"This is crazy," I tell myself. How is this my actual life? How did I end up here? Did I miss all the obvious red flags? Did I not look? Was I so naïve that I didn't see who was there the whole time? My mind feels like it's being ripped to pieces. This wretched flesh is begging for reprieve, but it never comes. Instead, wave after wave of soul-blackening grief. So much has died and it will only take a move of God, a real-life miracle, to fix this, to heal this, to redeem this. As much as I hate to admit it, I feel like I can't count on a miracle. It's not that I don't think God is capable, He is. But I can't even wrap my head around what a miracle would even look like. What would be the miracle here? What would a miracle look like in my life?

Undefined Miracle

It's easy for me to get caught up in defining my miracle, but what if it never happens? I'm left even further disappointed and fractured. Maybe the miracle is simply making it through this. Maybe the miracle is the daily strength and grace that God provides to hold it together, to be a kick-ass employee, and a phenomenal mother. I know we want to attach our hearts to a certain outcome, but we can't. This is the time to fight our flesh and what it wants, because what it wants may not be what it needs. I may beg God for a restored marriage when God is trying to protect me and my daughter from this broken person who is my husband. Only God knows the bigger picture.

This is so hard for me. Some days, I feel invincible. My mind is in a good place, my heart feels safe, and yet other days, I can't catch a break. I feel like I'm drowning. For whatever reason, this first week has been the hardest. My emotions are so raw. They have completely exposed my heart to all the elements, and I've cried more than I care to admit. It's that ugly cry, too, when you should call the paramedics in case you die from the pain. I've lost my patience and had to walk away from my dog or my child to cry. Making a bottle while sobbing my face off has been my go-to this week. Waiting for this undefined miracle feels like it's too much.

I've thought about this a million times, perhaps to the point of obsession, but what else do you do when your world turns upside down? What do I want? Do I want my marriage to work? Can I ever move forward and walk in full freedom from this anger? Will I not grieve everything that was lost? I will never be pregnant again with my first child. We can't relive those moments when he should've been supportive or loving, when he should've been there for me in every sense of the word. Instead, I remember his coldness. I remember every emotionally detached moment, when my soul was crying out to be known and completely loved, and I only found bitter rejection. Do I really want that back? Can people truly change that much?

I've seen marriages survive these brutal assaults on love. I've seen plenty of men and women make complete one-hundred-eighty-degree life pivots. Unfortunately, I don't think that's the person I married. The person I married is content with running away and avoiding his issues at all costs. The cost is me. The cost is my daughter. The cost is our family. It's insane that he doesn't see it. How can you be so self-absorbed that you don't see the immense damage you are doing to the people you profess to love? How is everything inside you not wanting to change?

So, what if things don't work out? What if he decides he doesn't want to try or that he doesn't love me enough to grow up? What then? I've obsessed over this option. I dream of being truly loved by a man, someone who I don't have to question his devotion to me. A man who is selfless and has integrity. Once I had a dream of being embraced by a man and feeling love simply in a hug. I woke up sobbing. I don't know what that is anymore. I feel nothing when he hugs me or kisses me and it's been a really, really long time since either of those has happened. It's so humiliating to be unwanted by your husband. I suppose it's natural for me to dream of being loved by someone else. I'm only human and we are designed to be in relationship. Every human wants to be known and loved. What do I do with all this? I can't decide what would be the actual miracle, but God does, and I must trust His plan and timing right now.

In the pages of this book, I'm going to be raw and vulnerable. I hope my vulnerability encourages you during this season. Find good people around you to help you navigate this, but you will do your best work alone. You will feel alone more times than not but know that many women have stood where you are. You can and will make it through this. This is life and sometimes it's cruel, but it's also painstakingly beautiful. You must learn to balance both. Let's dig deep.

    I do not intend to expose my husband. He will never read this book. I want to tell you it's okay. I've been there. And we're going to make it.

Chapter One: The Workout!

Alright, so now you know a bit of my story. After reading the first chapter, you either hate this book or are literally sobbing in the fetal position because you deeply resonate with it. Either way, I'm not sorry. The truth is you were drawn to this book for a reason. Let's figure that out, shall we? It's never enough to just read a book—there must be time to do the work. I strongly encourage you to take the time to reflect on the end of each chapter. Dig deeper to get know yourself better and figure out where you're at in this process of growth and healing.

You don't need another happy-ending book. I know I don't. I need a show-me-how-the-hell-I'm-going-to-survive-this book. That's what this is—brutal, gut-wrenching honesty and pain overflowing with hope for a yet-to-be-defined miracle.

Things to work out as you navigate vulnerability in this season:

1. Who have I allowed to be in my safe place? Did they earn this honor or am I dumping on or venting to them?

2. Have I sought counseling from a godly and reputable professional who can help me navigate my emotions healthily?

3. Have I told them the brutal, gut-wrenching truth or a watered-down version, so they don't pity me?

4. How am I taking care of myself right now?

SCRIPTURE REFLECTION:

"If any of you lacks wisdom, let him ask God, who gives generously to all without reproach, and it will be given him. But let him ask with faith, with no doubting..."

— James 1:5

"Loving ourselves through the process of owning our story is the bravest thing we will ever do."

— Brené Brown

CHAPTER 2

I'm Fine, Really

MOST DAYS I'M FINE. Really, I am. Then there are days when my heart and soul ache. I feel myself drowning in the tears I refuse to cry. I don't know if there's a greater pain than this one. Stuck in limbo, completely over feeling, and being rejected, yet still being rejected. What is this? I wish the tears would help me feel better, but they don't. Truth be told, I don't even know that having my husband come back will fix this. How does this wound heal?

I kicked my husband out of the house because I had to. I realize not everyone will be in the position to do this. I encourage you to find a way to get some time and space to yourself. It's nearly impossible to help heal yourself when you are constantly confronted with the trigger. Find somewhere you can go or agree to an arrangement where he leaves for a few days. I could feel myself going insane. My anxiety was through the roof, and even looking at him made me uncomfortable. I tried to carry this for so long that my body was deciding to shut it all down. I couldn't do it. Not to my beautiful baby girl. I can't collapse in this unbearable pain and quit. She needs me and she is keeping me alive in so many ways through this. As I write these words, I'm sobbing because it hurts so damn much. You never expect this to be your actual life.

I'm tired of pretending everything is fine, acting like my marriage is fine. Tired of numbing my emotions and burying my thoughts in stupidity. Where's my Hallmark movie? Where's the happy ending with the man who is crazy about me, who adores me, and who will do anything to make it work? I don't have that, and it makes me so sad and equally angry at God. It's okay to confess that out loud because it's the truth. I'm angry at God, but I know it's not His fault. My mind knows this, my heart knows this, still I want to blame Him. I can see Him sitting right in front of me, telling me "Do not fear." I want to cry all the ugly tears and not have to explain what part hurts the most because He already knows. I want someone to care about this pain. God is that someone.

Strong is all I have right now and most times I don't feel strong. I feel like I'm drowning, that I'm failing at life, failing at motherhood and friendships. There is such desperation in my heart for freedom from this internal prison. I hate that this happened. I hate that I can't control it or even decide an outcome. Listen, you can't control what happened to you, but you CAN control your response. There is ALWAYS a choice, and it's yours to make. File for a divorce? Sure, but does that really fix anything? And what about all this pain? For whatever reason, I wasn't enough for someone. I wasn't loved enough, wanted enough, even respected enough. Ugh! What a blow to your ego right?

You're probably thinking, "Girl, you are not fine." Given the circumstances, I am fine. I don't bump up against this hideous pain every day. I am working diligently at sorting through my various emotions, mainly disappointment and rejection. Disappointment has been the hardest for me to process. You must come to the place where you recognize what your expectation was. Disappointment only stems from unmet expectations. I had to examine what I was expecting and where that fell short and make peace with it. Obviously, strong emotions begin to manifest physically in our bodies—so I had to work those out. I bought a three-hundred-dollar treadmill off Amazon and got on it every day. Most days I walked and if I was pissed, I would run. It was incredible for my heart and mental health. I would throw on a podcast or listen to worship music and it was my time to do heart work. Recommend finding some way to pour into yourself DAILY.

I know we don't always have a ton of "me time" as parents, but the most important work you can do for yourself and your family is to touch base with yourself. Heal yourself. I am a huge advocate for therapy but unfortunately during this time, I don't have help with my daughter. So, I opted for self-healing. Some of my favorite books that have empowered me during this season have been *Girl, Stop Apologizing* by Rachel Hollis, *Untamed* by Glennon Doyle, and *The Body Keeps the Score* by Bessel van der Kolk. Reading saved my life. I mean it. You don't know what you don't know, and you need to educate yourself and read another person's perspective.

Most days I'm on top of this, practicing gratitude, focusing on my to-do list, and taking care of my daughter. Being a momma is HARD work. It's exhausting on so many levels and yet the most rewarding thing I've ever done. It's okay to be here, feel all the feelings, feel the hurt, and cry the big, ugly tears. Women get so good at stuffing down emotions until we get congested. Friend, I want us to breathe easy again.

I'm not trying to fake it 'til I make it and avoid my issues or pretend my pain doesn't exist. Let us honor our grief. We must sit down with our pain and get to a place where we can walk away from it. Our lives have experienced pain and things that, for whatever reason, we can't seem to walk away from. The scenario gets replayed a million times over in our head, obsessively analyzing how everything went so catastrophically wrong. I want to know why, how, and why again? I want to fix it, but I can't.

It's okay not to be okay. Don't stay there; you will be fine. Come to a place where you decide you win. If your marriage stays together, you win. If you end up getting a divorce, you win. I had to adopt this mentality to survive this shit storm. This philosophy makes sense because I'm going to grow as a person. Growth has become the number one priority for me and it should become yours too.

So how do you grow? Step one: DECIDE. Beachbody has the amazing motto Decide, Commit, Succeed. I love it because that's exactly how we need approach our growth. We need to decide we are going to do this, whatever "this" is. We are going to read the books, listen to the podcasts, find the time for therapy, invest in ourselves. Hear me when I say this—there is nothing more powerful than deciding. Most people are stuck in endless cycles because they won't make a decision. Decide you're going to do the work and grow through this. DECIDE TODAY.

When you're ready to move on to step two, stay committed. Commit to the process because it will be a process. You're not always going to be motivated to do the work. No one likes to face the music, no one. Commit to being temporarily uncomfortable so you can see something permanent. Growth, like healing, is cumulative. It won't be overnight but rest assured staying committed to your growth will yield incredible life -long results. Growth will bleed over to every area of your life. You will become stronger, more confident, and most importantly, whole. That is the goal here, Growth! That's why I say that no matter what happens, I win. Decide that in your heart. That either way, you win. Either way, you are not a victim, and you will learn, grow, and thrive no matter what. Commit to that.

Who Am I Kidding?

No one wants to grow up! We want the advantages of growing up like more wisdom, more stability, and better self-control, but we don't want to do the hard work of getting there. It takes a serious level of commitment to decide to be better, to change patterns and behaviors to reach the new you. I thought once you're an adult, that was it. You are who you are, and you do what you do. You won't change. For many people, that's true, but for the healthy person or someone who wants to be healthy, that's a lie. You can't stay

Half-Baked Love

the same. Different situations will demand a different version of you. Relationships will demand a different version of you. You need to demand a different version of yourself.

This process started with me really imagining my future. What kind of woman did I want to be? What did she look like? Think like? How did people describe her? If you can see it in your mind, you can definitely see it happen in your life. Who is the woman you want to become? Will you fight for her? Will you demand better from yourself to become her? You are not even the same person you were even a month ago so don't overthink how hard it will be to change. Subtle changes in your thoughts, small-degree changes in your behavior, better habits, etc. will manifest in better life choices. Everyone always thinks you have to make massive changes every day for results to happen, but it really is small changes that compound over time.

One of the best examples of this for me was my desire to not feel like the day was running me. I would let my child wake me up when she was ready to get out of her crib. So, I would already feel like I was behind and playing catch up. I just couldn't bring myself to wake up one or two hours before her because I would be exhausted. My desire to do better and have more "me time" was quickly snuffed out by thinking I had to automatically start at waking up an hour or two earlier. In my mind I had failed before I even started. You want to know why?

> **"Because you do not rise to the level of your goals you fall to the level of your systems."**
>
> — James Clear

You must do something that is going to work for you. There must be a system in place that is sustainable over time for you to win. I started with fifteen minutes earlier and when that got easier, I pushed more—thirty minutes, then an hour. Take small but sure steps to develop better habits.

You're probably thinking, "Why are you so focused on growth when your marriage is falling apart? Your husband is the one who needs to grow up." YES! You're right, he does. I can't continue to focus on everything he's not; how is that helping me? I can't spend one more day angry at all the selfish, immature things he's done. At some point you must decide to change your focus. Whatever you focus on only gets bigger. I decided that no matter what happens, I'm going to grow. I need to back up my decision with my commitment to that. Pastor Joel Osteen once said, "Life isn't happening to you, it's happening FOR you!" That's right, FOR YOU! This disaster can teach you so many things about life, marriage, relationships, God, and mostly about yourself. We are going to use this tragedy to grow into the best versions of ourselves every day. Do I mess up and say hideous things out of anger to my husband? YES, but I think the greater victory is all the things I didn't say that I wanted to say. Does that make sense?

The funny thing is he doesn't know that. He'll never know all the things I wanted to say that I didn't. What you say to people when you're hurting says more about you than it does about them. I could've cut him down, but I didn't say it. Today, I grew a little in self-control. Hey, I'm not an expert. I'm actively working on not being a vindictive b*tch when I'm angry at life and this situation. Exercising self-control to not say every unfiltered word I'm thinking when I'm thinking it is the hardest thing I've ever done. It's not that I want to be ugly about things, but for the love of God, sometimes they need to be said.

At least I think they do but truthfully, they don't. You will waste a lot of time repeating yourself to make yourself feel better. I can promise you that doing this will only make you feel better for about five minutes, and you'll be right back in the same boat again. It honestly would be better to journal those feelings out and see if you're making progress with it over time. Admittedly, this was one of my biggest mistakes repeatedly. I kept verbally exploding my emotions to someone who was in no place to hear me or help me. So, my frustration only grew, and it was my fault. I had to learn to exercise more self-control and hold my tongue.

I don't know that my ex ever cared about what I was saying. It would be foolish to assume in either direction—that he did or that he didn't. There wasn't any communication happening between us—just a lot of venting. To be clear, the entire point of communication is to gain understanding—that was not the case. I had no clue what he was thinking other than, "he's leaning more toward divorce." FULL STOP! What the hell? Does he think that's going to be easy? That divorce is the Mister Clean Magic Eraser and there will be no remnants of the damage he's caused? I don't get it. It makes me angry because what I really want is for him to take responsibility for his actions. Him saying he's leaning more toward a divorce feels like the easy way out. No one deserves this, and certainly not our children. I'm fully enraged writing this but I said nothing to him. I knew my words would fall on deaf ears and again I come face-to-face with my decision to grow and exercise self-control. I can feel my blood boiling because I don't understand selfishness at this level. I never want to be a person who can't consider others above self. I never want to be a person who refuses to grow up.

You know what other major feeling starts to rise during this process? Feeling like we are owed something. We need to talk about this because deep down this is what it all boils down to. Someone hurt us and we feel they owe us. They owe us our time, our lives, our happiness, our happy ending, insert what you're thinking. For a long time, I thought I wanted justice, but this feeling of being owed something is completely different. It is rooted in ego and a sense of entitlement. It's your pride that wants something. Ouch! You weren't expecting that right?

Look, I want him to step up to the plate and take full responsibility for his actions. That's what we all want right? But him taking responsibility will not fix feeling you are owed something. This was a horse pill to swallow. At the end of the day nothing he did or said would've changed that for me. He could have acknowledged that he destroyed something sacred for NO REASON other than selfishness. That there was NO excuse to do this to someone. It still won't mean or change a damn thing if you still feel like you are owed something. Don't let your entitlement get the best of out you. No one owes us anything. WE owe ourselves the life we want. If you are unhappy, you need to dig into the recesses of your heart and figure out why. Your partner needs to figure out why for themselves. This is an individual journey and a private process. Seek a professional to help you navigate this. Once you figure it out, communicate that to your partner and find a solution or goal to work toward or don't, ultimately the choice is yours.

I don't know your situation. I don't know why you picked up this book. Maybe a part of you resonates with being in a season of waiting. What you're waiting for may be different, but you're still waiting for the winds of change. You're still hoping for redemption, a fresh start, or a revived heart to beat again without feeling like you're drowning in pain. I think the waiting is the hardest part. You are on this journey, and you can't fully know what the outcome will be. Even if the choice is in your hands, you still don't know what the outcome is going to be. That's what makes this hard—this is where you need to have faith.

Chocolate Chip Cookies & Almond Milk

The Hallmark Channel is LIFE! I love all the sappy, romantic stuff, and when fall arrives, I can't help but glow waiting for Christmas movies to start. In fact, I look forward to fall every year because of the Hallmark Channel. My first year of marriage was different, though. I felt like there was something so desperately wrong and I couldn't put my finger on it. That year, I hated fall, winter, and the Hallmark Channel because I didn't have what those movie couples had. I didn't feel unconditionally loved; I didn't feel cherished or adored. Heck, I didn't even have a husband who wanted to have sex with me. I had to beg him, and it always felt so awkward and forced. He had no desire for me. It's obviously an act of God that I even got pregnant. If we had sex six times in two years, that's a lot, and that may even be an exaggeration.

I'm Fine, Really

If you are one of those women who does not particularly enjoy sex, maybe this is okay with you. You're exhausted from countless hours of full-time work, being a full-time mom, and sex is nowhere on your radar. I understand. But that's not me. I wanted to enjoy intimacy with the man I loved, but my husband didn't want me. I can't even explain how that devastated me as a human. I felt so completely disgusting to my husband. I've spent countless hours feeling ugly, worthless, rejected, and then stupid for wanting him to love me. It has been an endless torture cycle, trying again and again to feel accepted by him. My efforts were futile. There was nothing I could do to make him love me or want me.

Oh, my dear, my heart aches writing this because it is living torture for someone to do this to you. It is abuse in its highest form because it's silent. It wears down a person day by day by day, chipping away at the emotions that make us human. Eating away at a once self-confident person and now reducing her to nothing but rubble. Sex has now become something associated with shame and incredible rejection. There are so many things that I fear I will never truly heal from, this being one of them. How do you get over the love of your life not wanting you and rejecting you every day?

The answer may seem strange, but invite God into that space. The absolute truth about who you are, especially as woman, will trump your shame and rejection. I dare you to speak truth over who you are and what you were created to do on this earth. It was extremely comforting to know I am worth far more than rubies (Proverb 31:10). To remember that I am fearfully and wonderfully made and no matter who on this earth rejected me, God still calls me His beloved and I am His masterpiece. These become your affirming statements. Feelings cannot outrun TRUTH. The truth is you are so incredibly loved even on the days you don't feel it. God can and will heal even this.

It's been weeks now, and chocolate chip cookies and almond milk have been my dinner every night. I feed my daughter the very best organic meats, chicken, rice, vegetables, and fruit. Me, I eat cookies. It's kind of funny when I think about it. Because of dealing with high levels of stress, I'm craving all the comforts. Chocolate chip cookies are high on that list. It's exhausting doing everything by yourself. I make breakfast, lunch, and dinner every single day of the week. I have to clean up the kitchen, sweep, mop, take care of the laundry, clean bathrooms and bedrooms, walk the dog, take care of the dog, somehow keep this house in order, and in my "spare time," work on my personal growth. I'm tired, so exhausted. I survive on vanilla lattes with almond milk and occasionally a Cuban coffee.

I'm not saying this is the path, cause it's certainly not healthy or sustainable but it's what I did at the time to survive. Choose a workout instead. Lol! I'm kicking myself now cause imagine the killer body I would've had if I took that same dedication to my treadmill or lifting weights. Damn you, cookies. I'm kidding, sort of! Eventually after a few months, I snapped out of it and stopped eating the cookies. In fact, I didn't even crave a cookie for several months after that. Have grace for yourself, you really are navigating a lot right now. If a cookie gives you that temporary release of happy, eat a cookie but don't turn it into a lifestyle here. Choose better next time.

Being a mother with a broken heart during this season has been the most arduous role. I LOVE being a mother. God destined me to be a mother, and a damn good one at that. There is nothing I wouldn't do for my daughter. Nothing. She will always come before me and I will always have her best interest first, not mine. It comes as a shock to me that everyone doesn't operate this way. They boast they will do anything for their child, but when push comes to shove, they don't.

Being a mom or a dad is more than your title. I'm fighting for my marriage for the sake of my daughter and her wellbeing. I'm willing to push myself to the limit to grow and figure out how to improve our lives. I want her to know that she can overcome obstacles with hard work and dedication. Her father isn't like that; he's still stuck in his feelings. As a parent, you can't be like that. You must pull yourself together and put your emotions aside for the sake of your child/children. That is a major component of emotional maturity. You must be able to function regardless of your temporary circumstances. Your emotions SHOULD NOT be running the show. The flip side to this is knowing when to throw in the towel. Your emotions don't run the show, but they do need to be addressed. If you continue to just "function," I can guarantee burn out, or worse, a nervous breakdown. Being a healthy, good parent, is managing your emotions well and seeking help when needed.

Running Away from your Feelings

What are some emotions during this process? Everything and nothing and all that's in between. Most days you'll be fine, but every now and then you'll get a boulder of emotions to come crashing down on your head. I get triggered by rudeness (from my husband), annoying behavior (by my dog), and random crying for no apparent reason (from my child). If all these happen at the same moment, there is bound to be combustion. I mean, a woman can only take so much a day. Am I right?

I focus on managing my emotions to the best of my ability. I'm so thankful for this wonderful gift of grace. Grace isn't the ability to do wrong things and then expects to be forgiven for them. It's the ability and strength to do the right things in the here and now. I am VERY thankful for God's grace toward me in this season. It is not always easy to put a smile on my face, but I do it every single day and I even crack up laughing, too. After all, a cheerful heart is marvelous medicine (Proverbs 17:22). I don't want to be controlled by my emotions. I don't want my frustration, anger, and deep sadness to rule my days and affect how I treat others, especially my daughter.

It's okay to feel these things, and it's certainly okay to cry. But it's not okay to hold your child while sobbing with all your heavy, deep emotions. Children are fragile and very impressionable. Experiencing emotions is normal, but they haven't learned how to handle complex emotions yet. It's not fair to your child if you're having a meltdown every day in front of them. Learn how to control that. I became the master of a good, deep, big breath. I'm serious. When I felt like I was about to break, I would take a giant deep breath, close my eyes, and look up. Save that meltdown for naptime or give yourself a five-minute time out in your bathroom or closet. Do whatever it takes but DO NOT dump your emotions on your children. You are not a weak person and regardless of the situation, it will not crush you. Don't show your child that you are collapsing because life is hard right now. Let your child see a warrior rise and fight for their happiness. Don't let them see you giving up. Don't give up on yourself!

I give myself this pep talk at least once a day, and more often on those random, hard days. I'm not saying you can't feel all the things. There is a time and a place for it and it's not in front of your babies. Remind yourself that you are Wonder Woman in the flesh! You are fearless and brave! Sing all the silly songs, read all the little kid books, play all the games, and live your BEST life with them TODAY! You can't wait until you're feeling better to be their mom. Don't wait until you feel stronger to show strength. That happens TODAY. Right now. At this moment. Put the book down and go look at yourself in the mirror and tell yourself it stops today! I'm stronger and wiser than I've ever been. I'm going to show up for my kids and myself regardless of how I feel. I will not let my emotions rule my life.

As a woman, you have the innate ability to do this. I'm not saying it's easy. Breastfeeding is a natural thing, and it's hard as hell to get the hang of initially. But after a little patience and practice, you're a professional boob slinger and can feed your baby anywhere. It's awkward and you may ask, "Am I doing this right?" If you're managing your emotions and actively pursuing growth and peace, then YES, you are! Are you going to bump up against painful moments? Yep! Will your heart still hurt if you choose to manage your emotions? Absolutely. But you will be better for it, I promise.

I'm not even close to perfecting this craft. Around my daughter, yes, but get me on the phone with her father and have him say something stupid and I am a tornado about to touch down and destroy him. I hate when he affects me that much. UGH! Why? We already know why. Although my anger is justified, I'm not justified in disrespecting another human being because they hurt me. I can't intentionally hurt him and try to crush him. I'm better than that. I will not allow him to change me into someone I am not. I love people fiercely, am loyal, kind, and honest. I don't want to be or act like him.

The point is, we need to be consistently doing this, ladies! Let's show up for our babies and ourselves bigger and better than before. Let's get back on this mechanical bull and hold on for the crazy ride. Your legs are going to be sore as hell, bruises may occur, and that bull may inevitably throw you off. Get back up! We will not lie down and let an affair defeat us. We refuse to let any man determine who we are and what we are worthy of. The God of the universe made us in His image—we bear His seal of approval, and He says we are worth dying for.

Read all the books and find the time to do what's necessary to be the best version of you. I love reading and when I'm going through something, I want to read a book on the subject. I need to know how other people have overcome their obstacles. How do you walk through this successfully? Reading gives you access to knowledge you may not presently have, and it gives you some wonderful insight, too. Seize this moment and take it as a sign from God and the universe to grow up. Give yourself permission to grow. Be temporarily uncomfortable so you can accomplish something that's permanent. No one can take personal growth from you, ever. Your scars are yours alone to carry and sometimes they are badges of honor earned from survival that transforms you into the amazing woman you see in the mirror.

Don't Victimize Yourself

Hear me when I say this—you are a victim of circumstance, but you are not the victim of your life! You can't control what other people do to you, but you can control how you choose to respond and move forward. I know it hurts and being human sometimes manifests in finding someone to comfort you and tell you it's okay to be a victim. It's NOT, not even a little. You're not a victim. I'm not a victim. The actual victims are our children, but I will not tell my daughter that. She will grow up to be a victor, not a victim.

I don't know about you, but I can't stand people who make their lives always seem so much harder than yours. They must one-up every detail and make themselves be the victim in a romantic comedy while you are the living horror film. It drives me crazy. Yes, please tell me how hard your day was while your husband was working all day providing for your family, and how rude of him to ask you for sex, and your mom helps you all the time, and you have a nanny. Honey, I have friends with twins! What I am saying is you're NOT A VICTIM! Don't try to one-up me with your hard day or your hard life because I'm pretty sure I win. I will not sit there with you and paint a sorry picture so that you feel better. I don't see a sorry picture for my life—I see an opportunity to grow and change for the better.

Your mindset will determine so much in your life. If you victimize yourself, you will be powerless to help yourself move forward. We have so much more control than we think, and how we speak about situations affects a lot more than we realize. I know it's hard! Being a wife is hard, being a student is hard, getting a master's degree is hard, pregnancy is hard . . . it's all hard. We all get handed our own version of hard. It's a brand tailored to our life and our choices. Notice I said OUR choices because a lot of what's happening directly results from our choices. It's worth repeating—you can't choose what people do to you, but you can choose how you respond. Your response is so important! Don't be a victim.

Whew! Now that we've gotten that out of the way, let's sit down with a cup of coffee (or, in my case, a vanilla latte with almond milk) and think long and hard about our preferred future. Here's the thing—you can only control you. Your husband or boyfriend or whatever relationship you're in can't deter you from what you're trying to build for yourself. Of course, you want them there, ideally, but what about your life? Where are YOU going if they decide not to stay for the journey? I've been doing this for a while now. You must be careful with these thoughts. You're not fantasizing about your new single life; you are dreaming again about what you want. What are your goals? They can be new goals and new dreams, something that will empower you to grow and give you something to work towards. What is that very personal goal and dream no one knows about because you're too scared? THAT's what you need to think about.

Chapter Two: Things to Think About

I mean it when I say growing is the most important thing that you can do. This little limbo land of pain . . . you can go through it or GROW THRU it. You decide. I wanted to grow thru it as badly as I wanted to lose weight. I know that every time I wake up sore from the gym, I've torn through some muscle fibers and a powerful muscle is forming and growing. That temporary pain reminds me something new and stronger is about to be born.

This situation is the same—alas, more painful, but essentially the same. All the things you bump up against daily are reminders to go through it or GROW thru it. You get to choose how exciting (sarcastic) life will be, but also how exciting (totally serious) it can be.

Here are some growth reflection questions:

1. In the last six months, what trait(s) of yours changed for the better?

2. What is one area you want to focus on that needs a "grow-thru?"

3. How are you handling deep emotions when you're by yourself? With your kids?

SCRIPTURE REFLECTION:

"Count it all joy, my brothers, when you meet trials of various kinds, for you know that the testing of your faith produces steadfastness. And let steadfastness have its full effect, that you may be perfect and complete, lacking in nothing."

— James 1:2-4

"The amount of growth you will experience in your life depends on how much uncertainty you can handle."

— Thibaut

CHAPTER 3

It Is Well, Dear Soul

"**It Is Well**" **is** my favorite hymn of all time. It has been my anthem during this season along with a country song called "Worth It" by Danielle Bradbery. Both songs speak to how I'm feeling and encourage me, which is the point of most music. "It Is Well" encourages my soul. My favorite part is when it says ". . . whatever my lot, thou has taught me to say, it is well. It is well with my soul." Can you imagine how much faith it takes to get there? To accept that no matter what happens, everything will be well with you? I've come to the place in my journey of faith where I must choose daily to believe God and believe what He says in His Word. He will come through for me. It may not be how I want it to look, but I can trust that it is the BEST for me.

This is so hard, especially when you want to grasp desperately at the strings dangling in front of you. You want to call the shots and you want to determine what's best. If I'm being honest, I don't know what's best right now. I wish I did, but I'm learning to make peace with waiting and not knowing the outcome. I can tell you wholeheartedly I would not survive any part of my life without a relationship with God through prayer. I'm not a religious person and I don't use prayer as my I'll-pass-on-responsibility-and-not-deal-with-my life excuse. You know those people whose response is, "I'll pray about it," because they don't want to decide? I'm not that person at all. When I say I'm praying about it, I'm genuinely praying about it.

That's what I've been doing for over a year—praying. I'm praying for that undefined miracle. I'm praying for more wisdom and more energy. My toddler wears me out because she has the energy of a thousand suns. I'm praying for small miracles during the day—a longer nap, more creativity, expanded thinking to do my job well and be the best mom I can be. I want to do well regardless of what's not good right now. Prayer helps me get there. The more I pray, the more my heart changes. Things that were unbearable several months ago no longer have the power to bury me in grief. The anger I referenced earlier in the book has subsided tremendously. I'm not praying for MY outcome in all of this—I'm praying for the BEST outcome for everyone.

When I was single, I remember being in a season of loneliness. I would go to church every Sunday and come home sobbing because other members had a family. They all had someone they belonged to—they had children and seemed so happy and loved. I struggled with that because I didn't have a family of my own and I didn't know if it would ever happen for me. Fast forward a few years later—now I have a beautiful baby and a husband. Not the happy and loved part—at least not with my husband—but I don't feel lonely anymore. I would cry and pray to God (as many single women do) to give me a family. We want to build something beautiful and lasting; I think that's God's default blueprint for us. There is nothing wrong with praying to build something beautiful and lasting—a whole and healthy family.

During that season of singleness, I remember someone encouraging me to ask God to fill those empty places in my heart, the places that desperately wanted to be loved and wanted to feel known. I thought they were completely nuts. Ever since I got married, that has been my prayer. God, fill these empty places of hurt, rejection, feeling abandoned, unloved, unworthy, ugly . . . everything and anything. I let God into my life and personal plans. It's the most vulnerable I've ever been.

The pain can be all consuming and most days you won't be able to pick which part of you is hurting the most. On the days I can't decide what hurts the most, I end up angry. I remind myself to stop, take a deep breath, and pray. Ask God back into that space.

Does it all magically disappear when I say a brief prayer? Heck no, I wish! Sometimes I wish God was a genie. My apologies if that's disrespectful, or it offends. I know He's not a genie and I'm so grateful He's not. A genie would give you anything you want, regardless of consequence. God only gives excellent gifts. When you feel like He's holding out on you, maybe He is, but it's only because He has something way better.

What if you don't believe in God and prayer? What do you do in these situations to feel better? I know of a lot of women who pick up yoga, barre classes, and start taking long walks or hikes. Deep down we know we need to connect with ourselves and our Creator to heal; we need to pray. Everyone prays. You may not think of it as a prayer, and it may not be directed or attached to God, per se, but anyone in a season of waiting prays. Have you ever been in a tight spot and said, "Oh God, what am I going to do?" or "Oh my God, get me out of this!?" Believe it or not, that's a prayer. Who do you think hears you? Even your sigh is a prayer sometimes. I don't know what survival looks like apart from God and prayer. But I know God answers even the smallest of randomly addressed prayers.

Will There be Peace?

My unspoken goal in all of this is peace. I want peace. It would be nice to lie down and go to sleep at night and not wake up ten minutes later panicking. I don't want life to overwhelm me. You know that feeling—the one when you're slowing dying while trying to survive and fighting off every worst-case scenario. I want peace to reign in my heart and in my life.

Peace is such a beautiful feeling; circumstances in your life may be slow to change, but peace changes YOU—on the inside. You have peace that passes human understanding. I love the definition of peace in Merriam Webster's dictionary: a pact or agreement to end hostilities between those who have been at war or in a state of enmity. It also means freedom from disquieting or oppressive thoughts or emotions. I don't know how you feel, but my marriage is a war zone. More than anything, I want us to experience freedom from the overwhelming thoughts and emotions that want to defeat us.

As I mentioned earlier, I had to kick my husband out of our house. I spent a year trying to cope with this while trying to be a wonderful mom. I stuffed my emotions so deep I didn't even know I had them anymore. When it all came to a screeching halt, I thought I was doing well. Right around the time my daughter was ten months old, that postpartum fog lifted. I could see light again. My eyes opened to a whole new world, and in this world, I had to make decisions about the future. After several unsuccessful conversations and huge blowout fights with my husband about going to counseling, I couldn't deal with it anymore.

My anxiety was slowly coming back and taking over my life. If you've never struggled with anxiety before, you are now. It's okay—don't feel bad about it. Your anxiety is telling you something is up. You are not at peace within yourself, and all systems are blaring their alarms at you. That's all it is. Don't over complicate anxiety in this situation, because then you'll be handing over your control and power to it. I was anxious the minute my husband stepped into a room and couldn't settle my mind or emotions. My skin crawled, my heart pounded, and I thought I would surely pass out.

I was so angry with him, and no amount of time made those feelings diminish—they only got bigger. My body was responding to my head and heart. It was telling me HELLO VERONICA! You must deal with this! We can't carry on with you this angry. We must sort through these emotions. The problem was and is still there. So many! I didn't know where to start. I wanted to see a counselor but also felt cornered by my husband to not seek help. He wanted to bury all this underneath a rug and not face it. I couldn't anymore. There was no level of potential embarrassment that scared me enough to stay in this place. I wanted to shout this from the rooftop and take the power away from shame and embarrassment.

That's when I reached out to my friends. It saddened me so much to see their expressions and hear their thoughts, but all of them said the same thing to me, "You are so strong, and you will be fine no matter what happens." Thank you, friends! These words are still carrying me through this season. Having people who truly know you and love you, who can speak to your fear and doubt and say NO, you'll be fine was empowering. It's priceless. I finally told my family, and this is when I was the most embarrassed. I wasn't pretending everything was okay. I gave no indication how bad things were. They were heartbroken and angry, mainly because I chose to not tell them sooner and have their support.

I wasn't ready to tell anyone when this all happened. No one knew for almost a full year. I was gathering up my courage, forming my own thoughts, taking care of a newborn, and learning the ropes of motherhood. I didn't have time for someone else's feelings and opinions on my life. My marriage was a massive failure in my eyes, and I felt fully responsible. I was so ashamed that my husband cheated on me less than six months into marriage. In my mind, I reasoned it was all a reflection of me and believed the lie that I really am too difficult to be with. I made every excuse for him and why it was my fault. All that negative self-talk was robbing me of peace. It was destroying my peace.

There's such a tremendous weight of shame in all this, but I did nothing wrong, and you've done nothing wrong. Sure, we can be better and improve ourselves, but this level of betrayal isn't the result of who or what we are or aren't. I was so concerned with how this would look to other people. "OMG, she must be a horrible wife if he cheated on her already. Why? Maybe they don't get along? Maybe it's cause of the weight she's gained?" All the things went through my mind. I tortured myself daily for months. I was so scared of what people would think about me—never mind my marriage. What would they think about me? My husband fed these fears in a way to manipulate me into staying quiet.

I had my maternity pictures taken six days after my husband confessed his affair. SIX DAYS! My heart was broken, but I wanted to at least "look like a family." I wanted my daughter to see that she was (is) so loved and welcomed into this family. What family? (I'm bawling over here; my guts are ripping apart.) I put my strong face on and pushed through our pictures. Everything inside me wanted to have a meltdown and sob over my shattered marriage, over the lie that these pictures depicted. The pictures were beautiful though, and our photographer did a phenomenal job. In hindsight, although it may have been a show, I'm glad we did the pictures and I have photos of my pregnant belly and us together. I'm glad I didn't let my feelings run the show because I would have missed out on these pictures regardless of how bittersweet they are.

Solitary Confinement

There are so many things I would've done differently if I could. You may feel the same way. I would've told my mom sooner, I would've gotten help sooner, and I would have done a lot of things sooner. It pains me to think about the what ifs, so I don't. I waited and chose isolation instead. Not only was I dealing with this horrible marriage, but I also became a mother for the first time. I dreamed of this day forever and couldn't wait to hold my precious baby in my arms. Not once did I imagine it would unfold under these unfortunate circumstances.

There are many crucial events in a woman's life—losing her virginity, getting engaged, married, having a baby and motherhood. If I'm being honest, this robbed me of my dream of how these events would unfold in my life. Something was gravely wrong with my marriage from the beginning. I mean, from the wedding day. You only realize this after the fact. He hung out with his friends during the entire wedding. I had to find him to take pictures with our friends. Our wedding night? Crushing. We didn't even have sex on our wedding night. I cried myself to sleep; he passed out. If this wasn't a telling sign of what would come, I don't know what is. Honeymoon? No sex. I felt this huge disconnect and disappointment becoming my way of life. This man didn't want me. Why did he marry me?

I'd never felt more alone. Every newlywed is so happy they glow. They are living in marital bliss, and I was living in marital hell. My heart was so broken every single day because my husband constantly rejected me. The day I got pregnant, he only had sex with me because he was leaving for a few weeks. I was so ashamed and disappointed, but I didn't understand what was happening. Why wasn't I living the dream? I didn't even have a "honeymoon phase." The fights got bigger and bigger, and I was crying out for attention and love. He was saying I was too needy and didn't give him space. I resented him. How dare he make me live a sexless life? How dare he treat me like scum at the bottom of a pond? Who the hell did I marry? He's a monster! Then I found out about my baby.

I thought the news of us having a child would snap him out of this "funk" I thought he was in. Evidently, it didn't and well, you already know the rest. It's so unfair. How can someone who professes to love you treat you this way? I don't understand it. I withdrew deeper and deeper into myself, playing the game of "Everything is fine." My performance was Oscar-worthy. I even convinced myself that everything was going to be fine, that he'll change, and things will get better. What the hell was I thinking? Things went from bad to worse.

I can't explain the amount of heaviness in my heart as I write this, my chest weighed down by the emotional bricks laid one by one. I'm not healed from any of this as much as I wish I was. This is a deep wound that, with every cold shoulder, denied kiss, no affection and neglect, only grew deeper. I accepted his "version" of love for me. I said it was enough, that I could live like this, but no one can, and no one should. My isolation had me believing lies about marriage and about my own beliefs.

Isolating yourself is the WORST thing you can do in this season. I know it feels safe, and it gives you this false sense of security, but it will destroy you. Trust me on this. Please. Find a friend—a good and trusted, sound-minded friend—to help you navigate this. They will not have all the answers, but if they can, they will listen to you. Find someone who will encourage you. I cried on my friend's sofa so many times about how rejected I felt. She never knew he had an affair until months later when I couldn't take it anymore.

Your genuine friends will not judge you. Believe me, they will support you, and come alongside you, and hold your arms up. I get a visual of Rocky Balboa in the ring, exhausted, with his face beaten up. He goes to his corner and his coaches are holding his head up for him, giving him water, and wiping the blood from his face. This was me, but I chose not to have anyone in my corner for a while. This is a hard place to be, and it's okay if some days you don't have the strength to keep going. Call your friend. Pray. Do something that makes you happy and qualifies as "me time." I wish I would've done it sooner, but I was so scared, embarrassed, and ashamed of myself and my life and what it had become. If you're in this place and thinking this way, STOP. Find a friend you trust and spill the beans. Let it all out. Have some tissues and a glass of red wine ready. You can't continue carrying all this alone. You can't be the best version of yourself through this alone.

What happens when you tell all? You'll feel free! You've been giving all this power to shame and fear that when you finally let it out, you'll feel liberated! Beyond liberated, I felt loved by *my* people. I say "my" people because if you haven't figured it out yet, not everyone will be for you in this season. Being isolated will have you thinking all crazy. Find your people and reach out to them. Allow others to give you the love you deserve. Your girlfriends and your family will carry you through this season. If you don't have those, see a professional counselor. Don't feel ashamed to find help. Whether you're a mom in this season or not, it's still hard. You still need to be heard and loved through it.

Chapter Three: Things to Think About

There was a time in my life when I became addicted to the chaos. Chaos, struggle, and anxiety were a way of life for me. Once I truly discovered peace and learned to pursue it, everything changed for me.

I once heard a sermon where a pastor said, "Peace is a person." I thought that was a funny thing to say. Peace is a person, hmmm. Even though I'm not entirely sure it's what he meant, what I learned from it is that peace can go with you anywhere, much like a person can. You always have access to peace. Peace is not the absence of chaos in your life. Peace is a mental state, a spiritual state, and a practice. You practice peace. You pursue peace.

After everything that's happened, PEACE is one of my biggest priorities right next to growth. How did I do it??

Here are a couple of things you can try:

1. Wake up early before your household does, sit in silence, and think about all the things that bring you joy. Let yourself feel deep emotions of joy and happiness. Release the stress and the anxiety with every breath you take. Breathe in everything that's for you. Let go of expectations. Breathe in deeply and slowly. Feel that? That's peace.

2. Pay attention to how you feel when you leave a person's company. Your peace is a rare a precious gem to guard with your life right now. How do you feel after you hang out with certain people? Start paying attention to your emotions—who brings you peace? Who invokes feelings of calm for you? Stay close to those people and distance yourself from people who do the opposite.

SCRIPTURE REFLECTION:

*"In peace I will both lie and sleep;
for you O Lord, make me dwell in safety."*

— Psalm 4:8 NIV

"Peace begins when expectation ends."

— Sri Chinmoy

CHAPTER 4

To Divorce or Not?

YOU PROBABLY BOUGHT THIS book because you want to know the answer to this question. You want to know what I did, see how it worked out for someone else, and make your decision based on that. Well, let me tell you the hard truth—NO ONE can answer that question for you. You got yourself in this marriage and if you choose, you can get yourself out. I wanted someone to answer the question for me, too. Given everything you already know about this situation, what do you think? I think the answer is glaringly obvious—get the divorce. Yet, I still couldn't make myself to pull the trigger. Ugh!

I felt so much pressure from external forces to either stay and fight or cut the cord. "Veronica! Make a decision!" My head is spinning, and my heart is pounding. It feels so permanent, so much doom and gloom. My heart is breaking every day for what I feel will be an inevitable situation. Yet my dumb ass still wants to sit here and hope for the best. Ha ha! Sorry, I really had a chuckle there because that's the hopeful, cheery woman of faith in me. Dear Jesus, do something! Maybe He already did. Maybe the miracle is His strength to walk away with dignity.

Still, it hurts . . . this sinking feeling in the walls of your ribcage. The feeling that says your life is going to change, and it's going to hurt even worse than it already does. I'm scared that my daughter won't be okay, and I won't be okay, but I can't focus on that. I know we both will, I have faith that we will. In fact, we will be better than okay. I do fear this pain getting worse. I can't tell you how hard it is to carry this every day, but if you're reading this, you already know. You are there—you are right here with me in this pain—or you know someone who is. It's awful, and for as much support as I feel, I feel equally displaced. I never imagined myself being a single mom.

If you're in this place and you don't have kids, in a lot of ways, you are in an easier position. You only have to consider yourself and not the wellbeing of another human. I'm not taking anything away from the heartbreak and pain of this because the pain is real. The silver lining for you is there are no children involved. I love my daughter so very much and I am beyond sad for her in all of this. She is the reason I cling to hope. The only reason.

Call It as You See It

I can be hopeful all day long, but at some point, I have to call it as I see it. I'm over here sacrificing—paying every house bill alone, supporting my daughter in every sense of the word, and her father is living his best single life—while still very married. I can try my best to be optimistic about that and say this behavior is helping him de-stress. Maybe he's getting things out of his system. Maybe he doesn't know how to respond. Maybe. Maybe. Maybe. Or maybe it's all bullshit and I need to pull my head out of my ass.

There are a lot of things I love about myself—one being how fiercely loyal I am—but in this exact moment, I also hate that about myself. Why am I being loyal to my absent husband? Everything (and I really mean everything) he is doing screams "I DON'T WANT TO BE WITH YOU! I will not change and make this work. I choose ME!" The hardest pill to swallow is always the bitter truth. If he wanted to make this work, he would. If he wanted to be part of a family and be a healthy family, he would do the work to deal with his issues and make amends. He's not doing any of those things. I face the heart-wrenching decision of divorce or no divorce.

Here's what I don't want. I don't want to keep holding on to false hope, allowing months and years to go by, causing further damage. I don't want to play house for the sake of my daughter because I never want her to think this behavior is normal and that this kind of relationship is okay. It's not! If I want my daughter to recognize and choose good options for her life, it means I must choose better options for myself. With children, more is caught than taught. Who do I want to be during and at the end of this challenge? Who will my daughter see? I want her to see a warrior rising from the ashes. Life may try to beat me down, but I will rise.

So, what about you? Did that help you make your decision? Probably not. You can't base your decision on my life and feelings. You must do that deep heart check yourself. I can't tell you what to do. I don't know what's best for you. If you are in a dangerous or abusive situation, I emphatically say YES, GET A DIVORCE! If you think finding a counselor and therapy will help, do that. Exhaust all your resources before you pull the plug. If your partner is unwilling to cooperate with you, you really don't have another choice.

Sometimes I am so embarrassed. I'm begging and pleading for my husband to pick me. I dread that feeling because someone who loves you picks you automatically. You don't have to tell them what's great and worthy about you. They already know.

Why do I keep asking him to reconsider? Why? Because deep down, I love him, and I want our marriage to work. However, the brutal reality is he doesn't love me and does not want to make this work. I must pull the plug, cut the cord, and cut my losses. I regret it has come to this, but how long should you wait for someone to choose you? The answer—you either know or you don't know. There really is no in-between. I've allowed myself to remain in limbo over this.

Oh, The Church

Sadly, in my experience, the church has missed their opportunities to support broken families. I'm not speaking of one specific church—I'm referencing the Church at large. I've seen many women shamed into staying married to their adulterous husbands. I've seen many women chastised for not loving a broken person enough to wait for God to heal them. I've seen church leaders use their position to overpower what was the healthy, logical choice in all of this. I've also witnessed how shunned the divorced, single mom is. That hurts the most. I don't want anyone to treat me differently, and I certainly don't want my daughter treated differently because of her father's decisions.

It's bound to happen. Someone will say something so ridiculously insensitive, "Well, did you try counseling? Have you prayed about it? Have you fasted?" I'm laughing out loud because I want to be the sometimes rudely sarcastic person I am and say, "No, I didn't even try any of those things yet. OMG! Thank you!" If you know me, you can hear my tone saying this. Not nice! These people mean well (at least I think they do) but seriously, stop! I'm pretty sure no woman alive signs up for divorce and waves her hands wildly in the air, saying, "PICK ME! I want a divorce!" Let's be real—this isn't what we planned for.

All my church folks—want to know how to support someone in this season? DON'T talk about their failed marriage and cover it with your "holy cloak" of "let's pray for them." I've been in church my entire life. I've seen how this plays out more times than I care to admit. Be supportive of their decisions regardless of whether it's not supporting your opinion. My pastor does this well. She has been incredibly supportive of my thought process and has never said a judgmental word about it. She simply says, "I'm here for you, whatever you decide." That's all a person needs in this situation—someone to say, "I'm here for you. When others walk away, I will be here for you. I'm here to offer you a mental break, watch your kid for a couple of hours, bring you dinner, or a latte. Or I can come over and watch a movie with you, so you don't feel so alone. What do you need? How can I help you through this?"

We appreciate your prayers but remember to think practically. How can you help a single mom? How can you help someone who's been married for decades when their husband suddenly walks out on them? Or you're the one who walks out because you won't take the abuse anymore and you've decided you want more and better for your life. Be supportive, regardless of the reason someone goes through a divorce. Marriage is hard work. I wish I had my fairy tale happily ever after. It doesn't look like I'm going to, and instead of telling me to try harder, say something encouraging, "No matter what, you will overcome this. You and your baby girl will be fine." Don't shove scriptures down my throat about praying for my husband. I have biblical grounds for divorce.

Not every church is like this. There are some wonderful churches that have divorce recovery groups, single mom groups, and singles group. They understand that humanity is fractured, and we all need some love and encouragement. Thank you to those churches that are supporting their members. It's difficult being in a taboo group. Divorced single moms carry negative social weight. It's a title people use to define who I am. I won't let it! Don't let it define you either. If you choose to get a divorce after you truly given it your all, you've done your best! Be proud of yourself for what you've accomplished and hold your head held high. You've endured trauma and betrayal and you're still alive to talk about it. Be proud of how far you've come.

The "D" Word

I'm seriously confused about why divorce is such a taboo thing in the twenty-first century. Half of all marriages end up in divorce. HALF! In some places around the globe, the percentage is higher. That tells you something about the state of the world. People are struggling to have healthy relationships. Divorce is not the "D" word. Disappointment is! The struggle isn't about getting a divorce or thinking about getting a divorce. I'm struggling with my disappointment! This is my marriage, and I am disappointed. I'm disappointed that this is the person I married. I'm disappointed in myself for a million reasons.

Today I had the distinct memory of my husband's proposal. I remember saying yes and instantly feeling a pit in my stomach. I thought I was scared, but maybe in hindsight it was my gut response saying NO, he isn't the one. Man, I want to slap that version of me. After all that I've been through, how did I miss that? I was racing to the altar, and for what? To fit the social norms of living in the South? Was getting married in my thirties really that bad?

Yes, there is so much to be disappointed in. Don't let people make you feel divorce is doomsday if that's what you decide. You're not a failure because you're thinking about getting a divorce. Other people aren't living your life and ultimately can't help with your disappointment. You'll have to make peace with that on your own.

It's No One Else's Fight

The reality is simple—it's no one's fight but your own. People will have opinions all day long. Some will be for divorce, and some will be for working it out. You might feel the same on any day. You might bounce back and forth repeatedly and feel like a crazy person. It's a big decision—as big as getting married. It all feels so permanent, and it sucks that suddenly forever got cut short. Whatever you decide, it's your choice. I know how hard this decision is. I also know that most days I avoid even thinking about it because it weighs so heavily on my mind and heart. Maybe you're not in a place to decide yet. That's okay! It's okay to wait a little longer and see how things are working out.

Don't feel rushed into a decision that will affect you forever and your kids (if you have them). I think that's the hardest part for me right now. Everyone is saying "Get a divorce! What are you waiting for? He's never going to change, and he clearly doesn't want to grow up." I know all these things, but it doesn't make it any easier to make that decision. Love defies logic, and for whatever reason, I keep hoping it's going to change magically. Maybe that's you too and there's nothing wrong with that. Don't feel bad for hoping love will ultimately win. Love is supposed to win, but this time, it may not be on this side of eternity.

It has been most helpful to establish timelines in my mind. For example, after he confessed his affair, I said to myself, "Okay, I'll give him a year and see if he does anything to work on himself and his issues. I'll work on myself and in a year reevaluate." Well, that year came and went, and nothing changed. I take that back—a lot changed, and it got way worse. As much as I wanted to work on myself, I didn't have the time, the emotional or mental energy. As a new mom, I was always exhausted. Everything went from bad to horrific in a few months. I'm sure it's not an exaggeration to say we hated each other. At the very least, we resented each other.

It's not healthy for anyone to live this way. I'm not saying it's the reason to get a divorce. It's a reason to reevaluate and reflect on what's happening. Many people recover from affairs. If you recover and do the work on making marriage work, you will be better for it. Either way, you grow! I hope you're married to someone humble, one who values growth, will do the work, and can admit when they are wrong. I hope you're humble and don't let pride be your false sense of security. We do not waste love. If the relationship ends, you still learn something.

Hear my heart when I say this—marriage is worth every ounce of fight you have in you. It's worth trying everything you can. I'm not telling you to give up. If you have a sliver of hope in your heart, hang on to it for dear life. If you still have faith that a miracle can happen, water that seed of faith. This is your fight alone and no one, not even someone walking the same journey, can tell you what's right for you. Choose what you're willing to fight for or make peace with. It's all up to you! Whatever you decide, don't feel bad about it!

I'm no expert in this season. I'm learning how to navigate this journey, too. There's no way to predict what life will look like six months from now or even a year from now. I want to be hopeful and hang on to that sliver of hope as well. But I'm tired and worn out right now. Nothing on the horizon looks positive. All I see is his busy schedule, with most of it out of town, and no intention of having a conversation about this.

It's not fair to keep another person in limbo. If you are the person keeping someone in limbo, stop. It's not fair! If you need more time to process and think, say that, but set a timeline or deadline and talk about it then. You can't continue to let time slip away with no conclusions. Even if you need more time, say so. Don't you dare be the person who's going to exercise revenge on this. There is no revenge here. No one wins when the marriage fails and being petty and immature will not make you feel better. In fact, you'll only feel worse. Sure, it's gratifying to say mean things in the moment, but you feel terrible afterwards. Again, don't let your emotions run the show. You are the ringmaster. This is your circus, so keep your animals in check.

Create Safe Places

This is one of the few reasons I think I'm still sane. I've worked hard to create safe places for my thoughts and my heart. A lot of those safe places are very kind, wise friends, and the other is what I'm doing now—writing. Writing has become my outlet for all this pain. The countless thoughts and emotions get typed out either on my laptop or on my iPhone. You don't have to share it with anyone, but let your vent happen. It's so important to release the pain in this season. You are not an island, and no one is expecting you to not have hard or bad days. In fact, I'm sure they expect the opposite, and they are waiting there for you. I'm thankful my friends know me and understand my personality. I'm not the person who needs to vent every day, but I also don't need to be queried daily with, "How are you? What are you feeling today? What do you think is going to happen?" I appreciate the concern, but I don't need to provide daily briefings.

You need people who will check in on you from time to time, but mainly people who will help your life proceed as normal. Normal hang time, coffee time, movie time, play dates with the kids, drink wine, or anything else your heart desires. I speak for anyone in this situation when I say we don't want people to feel sorry for us. We're not sad pity cases. If you want someone to feel sorry for you, then please re-read "Not Being a Victim" section of chapter 2. I won't feel sorry for you! This sucks and I know this hurts, but I will not pity you into staying stuck where you are. Find a safe place to vent and heal and grow. Be okay with knowing that your partner may not appreciate your safe space. Most men don't vent and keep everything private.

Find a therapist or counselor if your friends don't do it for you. A therapist or counselor will do wonders for your mental and emotional wellbeing. There is a lot to process, and they can help you navigate that in a healthy, productive way. I know it costs money, and maybe you don't have the funds, but try to schedule at least two sessions and be honest with them. Let them know you don't have the money right now but see if they will offer a free initial consultation to assist with resources for books to read or programs offered to women in crisis. Additionally, there is online therapy through programs like BetterHelp.com or TalkSpace. Something is better than nothing.

You need to heal from this betrayal and grief. Don't "get by" and avoid it because you don't want to be in the same place mentally and emotionally years from now. You want to grow, change, and be a whole person. It's your responsibility to do the work, so don't put it off thinking it's going to be too hard or too painful. It may in fact be #allthethings, but it will also feel so amazing when that pain isn't there anymore. I wish we could all be in a room together right now, give each other hugs, and tell each other how brave and strong we are. You will get through all of this and be stronger and better on the other side.

What else can you do in your safe place? Create something new. I am excited to dream again about a new future. It is so important to have something to focus on in this season. It can be whatever you want. You might join a yoga studio, book club, mom's night out, or girl's night out, write a book, or record an album. Do whatever is going to be healthy and make your heart happy again. It will be so therapeutic for you to get excited about something. Confession time: I've been trolling the Internet for a new puppy! Hahaha! I LOVE DOGS! I am intensely obsessed and want to pet every dog I see on the street, give it a kiss, and let it lick me. Did I mention I LOVE DOGS? I'm happy to report that my daughter is the same—she LOVES them!

Then I remember how hard it is to train a puppy, that they pee and poop everywhere until they are house trained, and it all passes. LOL! Guess I'll continue stealing snuggles from random dogs in the streets. The point is it makes me happy! Dogs are some fiercely loyal creatures, and their love is unconditional. We don't deserve such wonderful animals in our lives. They are the best! Find something that's going to light you up again. Dealing with a divorce is heavy, and it sucks the soul right out of you. Be happy even at this time of waiting. Happiness is a choice, and it is an inside job. You have the power to choose happiness amid chaos and deep sadness.

Workout

I'm the last person signing up for a workout but the first person to tell you, "You need it." It is so good for your mental health to exercise every day. If you can't do every day, try every other. Get your body moving and free it from that funky energy. Energy transfers to people all around you. What are you transferring to people? What are you putting out there? Doing a workout challenges me not only physically but mentally. I am going to make excuses for not doing a workout or I will train myself to push harder even when I don't want to. That is worth the lesson.

I do T25 by Beachbody. I love it! It's so challenging and most days I'm with the moderator of the video, but at the end of it I'm drenched in sweat, and I swear I'm already skinnier. We feel better after a workout! If you're having trouble sleeping, regular exercise will help. Also, drink more water. Find a workout you can do at home or go to the gym and work it on that elliptical or treadmill. There are several free workouts on YouTube. I don't have a babysitter, so I work out in my basement. It's the best twenty-five minutes of my day. It's another thing you can do for YOU that has tremendous benefits and gives you that extra boost of endorphins needed to survive this level of crazy we've got going on.

We are in a hard space right now. We don't know whether things will work out and we don't know if we want them to either. That may not be how you feel, but it's how

Half-Baked Love

I feel. I don't feel confused—I feel really torn with all this. I don't think there's a right or wrong answer here. It's what can you live with and be at peace. It deserves your attention because it will change everything.

Chapter Four: Things to Think About

DREAM AGAIN.

My goodness, I want to shout this from the rooftop! Imagine your new future life with happiness. Imagine it with you smiling, feeling peace, picture the friends, your kids (if you do or don't have them). What does your preferred life look? This might sound such a crazy thing to say during a time this, but I promise it will keep you going. It will keep hope in your heart that things will get better. Even though you're experiencing a loss right now, your future can still be a giant WIN.

Here's one thing I did (that I still have) and I encourage you to make one, too.

MAKE A DREAM VISION BOARD.

If there were no limits on time, resources, energy, etc., how would your dream life look? The house, the car, the clothes, your character, encouraging words or phrases. Don't worry about making it pretty make it meaningful. Put it somewhere you can see it every day. It will surprise you how many of those things will start coming into your life. Manifesting is real. Throw your energy at positivity and you will get positivity right back in many forms, many times over.

Let's Make that Vision Board
(It can be a digital vision board, too)

Digital or not, these are the elements needed. If it's digital, find images or word graphics online.

1. Create a list of goals or thing that you would like to see happen this year.

2. Find pictures or words that inspire you and represent your goals.

3. Make a collage either on a cardboard poster or digitally using apps like Canva or Unfold.

4. Make sure to include affirming words you can read to yourself every day.

5. Make it visible DAILY. Make it your wallpaper on your phone or hang it up around your desk. It will remind you where you want to go and keep you focused on getting there.

"You are never too old to set another goal or to dream a new dream."

— C. S. Lewis

CHAPTER 5

The Sorry You'll Never Get

THERE'S A BOOK WRITTEN by Gary Chapman called *The Five Languages of Apology*. I highly recommend you read it. It provides five languages or ways to handle apologies. Why does this matter? Because someone may apologize to you but you can't accept or hear it because it's not in your language. I think that's the case for me. The five profile types are Expressing Regret, Accepting Responsibility, Making Restitution, Genuinely Repenting, and Requesting Forgiveness. I encourage you to read this book and figure out your type. There is a free test online to figure out your language type. Google the title and you'll see the link for a free profile test. Want to guess what I am?

My highest score was in Accepting Responsibility, and the second highest was Expressing Regret. It did not surprise me at all. This is all I'm wanting but clearly not getting because I don't believe my husband is sorry. If he is, he's not speaking my language. Another book you should read is *The Five Love Languages* by the same author. Reading influential books will be your saving grace. Not only will they help you grow, but it'll entertain your brain with good things. You can't fix what you know nothing about. I'm passionate about being informed. We live in the age of information. Ignorance is NOT bliss. Educate yourself about the things that mean the most to you.

My husband and I finally had the pow-wow I've been waiting for and, as usual, it didn't go well. The only thing notably different was I didn't feel the need to attack him. At some point, you must accept what is, and this is a broken marriage with two people who are hurting in similar yet distinct ways. This is an enormous step in the right direction. I realized that although he did not communicate the apology in a language I understand, it's his apology. Does that erase everything that happened? Hell no! I wish it was that easy.

The other thing I'm learning to make peace with is the apology that may never come. This is hard because the way I receive an apology best is when the other person accepts responsibility for their actions. If I don't believe they have accepted responsibility, then I don't believe they've apologized for anything. What about you? Have you received the apology you've been waiting for? Have you received the apology you've needed to move forward? If the answer is yes, fantastic! If your answer is no, that's okay, too. I'm right there with you. It has a lot to do with your language of apology, or maybe there's been no apology. I've said this for as long as I've been alive, but sorry doesn't fix it; actions do.

You might need to move forward without an apology. I know it's hard and so unfair, but your peace of mind is worth more than words. I'm not saying it's not important, it is. I know it is because, as a woman, I want my husband to acknowledge he hurt me in ways he can never repair. We can't go back in time and do it all over again. I want him to own that fully, and if the weight of that feels crushing for a time, so be it. Our decisions weigh heavily on us, good and bad. Make conscious decisions and be aware of how it's affecting those around you.

Forgiveness

Let's talk about something that is not popular, especially considering an affair. Forgiveness. While some well-meaning people will tell you, "You don't have to forgive him or her," the truth is you do. It doesn't have to be today or tomorrow. It may take you a long time to get there, but you still must do it. Another book recommendation for you is *Forgiving What You'll Never Forget* by Dr. David Stoop. This book helped me tremendously in navigating this journey toward forgiveness. If you're not a big reader, it's not that long of a book. You can read it in a few days.

Another thing I've struggled with in this journey of forgiveness is the forgetting part. Well, good news! As human beings, it's impossible for us to forgive and forget! YAY! I don't know about you, but that came as a massive AHA moment of my life. The reason is simple—the things that cause you trauma in life also serve as life lessons. If you were to forget the lesson, you might have to relive the trauma. As bad and as ugly as being cheated on and having your marriage fail is, it's teaching you something about the world around you. It's showing you who your genuine friends are, who you are, who God is in all of this, and who you want to be. These lessons are invaluable regardless of how they present themselves. I was so stuck in wondering how I would ever forget this, and it's such a tremendous relief that I don't have to forget it. That doesn't mean I keep reliving it over and over in my head. It simply means that it's a part of my past and what happened. Honor the place it had in your life and everything it taught you and continues to teach you.

I've always known that forgiveness is a journey, and I certainly didn't expect it to come overnight. Did you know that it's always an immediate decision? Think about that—once you say or decide to forgive, it's immediate. Living that out is the actual journey. Let me clarify this a bit—a few weeks after his confession, I told my husband, "I forgive you." That doesn't take away from how angry and hurt I am. It diminishes nothing done in the past or how I'm going to live the rest of my life with this knowledge. None of that goes away. Yet, saying "I forgive you" out loud tells my brain and mind something. It says I can do this, I'm willing to walk this out with you, and I will not hang this over your head. Is it easy? HELL NO!

Until this point in my life, every time I've forgiven someone, it's been relatively easy to move past it. This seems damn near impossible most days, but I am working on it. Forgiveness has nothing to do with my husband. It's all on

The Sorry You'll Never Get

me. It's my choice to forgive the offense and the trauma. That doesn't take away from anything that happened. It means I will not hold this against you. As women, we all have the tendency to keep offense in a file folder that we pull out during an argument or heated discussion. We've all been there. Trust me. However, someone who's growing in maturity, empathy, and in learning how to love won't do this to someone else. It doesn't look good on you, sweetheart.

I did an inner healing session once, which I won't go into much detail about other than to say it brings a lot to the surface. One thing it brought up was this notion that I felt my husband owed me something. It was such a deep and alarming truth to hear. I really believed my husband owed me something, but I'll never get back what was lost. I'll never get back time that's passed. I'll never recoup my first pregnancy and not feeling emotionally supported. There's so much restitution that's never going to happen. This thought of being owed something shook me, so much so that I could barely get the words out of my mouth to say, "you owe me nothing." This sent me into hysterics. My emotions were in a very high state, and I was bawling like a child throwing a tantrum. Saying out loud that my husband owed me nothing was nowhere near the truth of how I felt.

I wanted him to redeem everything, everything that I was grieving, which cannot be done. How dare he ruin this marriage! How dare he shatter every thought and beautiful expectation of how I thought our lives would play out! How dare he destroy everything I held dear and sacred! I'm not wrong about feeling my husband owes me something. But that's not forgiving someone. Ouch! I feel that in the pit of my stomach. I know you want to do the right thing in this, the mature thing. It's difficult when you can't get past this major hurdle of feeling you're owed something.

Cancer of Your Soul

I know cancer is a very strong word, and it scares people, rightfully so. But did you know that when you choose not to forgive, it gives you soul cancer? You're probably thinking, "Wait, what? Veronica, you're getting weird." When you don't forgive someone, all those emotions transform into other negative emotions. If you continue to feel you're owed something and never get it, you'll resent him/her. Resentment will go back and forth between anger and bitterness. Bitterness will become unadulterated hatred in your heart for that person. That hatred will eat away at your soul, day by day by day, until there is nothing left of you. You will hate your life, disconnect from people, people will distance themselves from you, you will become toxic to the world around you, and your soul will have cancer.

I'm not being dramatic when I say that. I have seen this happen time and time again in the lives of people I care about. Your negative emotions are toxic and can change the chemistry of your brain. Dr. Caroline Leaf has several books talking about your thought life and how it affects you. The one I recently read is *Who Shut my Brain Off?* This book highlights the thought process and what it does to your brain. Negative emotions and thoughts are literally TOXIC to your body. Imagine carrying them around long enough that you end up with cancer.

Let me clarify—not everyone who has cancer or will

get cancer is a result of their negative emotions or thoughts. That's not what I'm saying here. What I am saying is that your thought life does and will absolutely affect your body and your body's chemistry in the long run. There's a verse in the Bible that says, "Be very careful about what you think. Your thoughts run your life." (Proverbs 4:23 MSG) It may not be today or next year, but keep it up long enough and you will note the change yourself. If you have a loved one dealing with cancer or someone who passed from cancer, let me offer my sincerest condolences. Cancer really is such an awful disease, and it doesn't discriminate. I am in no way, shape, or form making light of it, so please hear my heart on this.

My sister was diagnosed with a rare form of neuroendocrine tumors (NET cancer) early this year. She was one week postpartum when they found out and our lives were all turned upside down. On top of dealing with my personal hell, I was deeply saddened and afraid for my sister. Thankfully, the doctors caught and dealt with it in record time. She is now cancer free, missing about 2/3's of her right lung, but she's alive and that's all that matters. I know from personal experience what it's like to see someone deal with something they can't control. Everyone rallies around them to pray and hope for the best possible outcome. Your thoughts are within your control! Don't let your family and friends see you spiral into a deep, dark grave of unforgiveness. It's not worth it for anyone, especially you.

You are so much better than this and, trust me, you are stronger than you think. You absolutely have the power to choose forgiveness in this situation. It doesn't mean you have to reconcile anything, and it doesn't mean you have to stay or go. It simply means you are forgiving the offense and releasing the power it has over you. It's one hundred and ten percent for you alone. You can have peace in your heart, and you can heal. It's up to you alone if you want that for yourself.

Now Walk it Out

How many of you instantly heard that song in your head? Just me?! LOL! (It's by a group called UNK. Google it.) How do you walk out this journey of forgiveness? I'll be the first to tell you it's difficult, but it's doable. I want to cite an example of another traumatic event in my life to show you how forgiveness played out. In my early twenties, I was raped by someone who attended middle school with me. It was, and still is, the biggest blow to my faith in humanity to date. A lot of life has happened since then, but on a personal level, that was severe.

Talk about trauma and recovering, that will do it for you. I had debilitating social anxiety and PTSD, enduring severe stomach issues from being so terrified and anxious all the time. I lost about thirty pounds in a month; I was heavier then, so it was fine. I was so anxious I couldn't eat, and when I did, it would send me running to the bathroom to either vomit or have diarrhea. It obviously was an extremely traumatic event.

I remember meeting with the prosecutor and having to retell the story a million times. I was so embarrassed, and I had to explain it all to men, no less. It was the WORST! The absolute WORST! After a very long, grueling interview discussing all the details, I said, "You know what? I don't want to do this. I want to forgive him and move forward with my life. I don't want to relive this event over and over for the next year or however long the process was going to take." At that moment, I forgave. I said it—it was simple, and I didn't complicate it. I knew it was within my power and control to offer such grace to someone, and I did.

Does that mean I picked up the phone to tell him? Does that mean we became friends and hung out months or years later when I was over it? Ummm, that's a firm no. It doesn't mean any of those things. It means I'm no longer mad or angry about it. It means I did the work and got the counseling and therapy needed to heal from a traumatic, violating event. If his picture pops up as a suggestion on Facebook, I don't cringe or feel sick to my stomach. The offense is removed, and I don't hold it against him. This is not a hypothetical situation—this is real life. That's not to say that if we were in the same room, it wouldn't be awkward. It could very well be the most uncomfortable experience ever, and with good reason. The trauma taught the lesson. There it is full circle! You can forgive, but you won't forget.

Do the work and walk in forgiveness. It is freeing beyond what you can imagine, and you'll be glad for it. This situation doesn't have to dictate another second of your life if you don't want it to. You have the power to choose in this moment what you want. I'm hoping you choose to forgive. As hard and as irrational as that may seem, it's your first step toward healing. Remember, we can't control what people do to us, but we can control how we respond. You want to be free from this weight in your chest that makes you feel bad. I've been there so many times, so many. I can tell you from firsthand experience that forgiving someone is worth it. It's always worth it and will benefit you tremendously.

Your life lessons are cumulative. If you forgive once in a hard situation, you are more likely to do it again. If you show grace once, you'll show grace again. There's nothing wrong with choosing to be a better version of you. It does not have to make sense to anyone why you forgave someone. It does not need to be shouted from the rooftop. That's between you and God. If you've truly forgiven someone, it will be demonstrative, especially if that person remains in your life. It's a journey—if you've already said you've forgiven someone and then you have an enormous blowout fight, it's okay. Those are the parts of you that are not healed yet. Those are the things you need to work on. You don't have to crucify yourself for being human. Try harder next time.

Sometimes the victory is in the things I didn't say, and that's true here again. You will bump up against this again and again. You will get triggered by things and when you are, you have the choice. Either you can get ugly, or you can extend grace. You can be crazy, or you can practice walking out forgiveness. It's your choice. It's always going to be your choice. I want you to feel empowered to make good choices, even in the middle of this tremendous tragedy. We live in a very broken world, and everyone is dealing with something. We all need help. Don't be afraid to ask for it and/or seek it out.

Chapter Five: Things to Think About

I've heard this my entire life: "Forgiveness is setting a prisoner free, only to find out the prisoner was you." OUCH.

Betrayal is the hardest thing to forgive. Hands down, no contest. Why? Because we believe the other person deserves every horrible thing in life coming for them and they certainly don't deserve our forgiveness. I know, I know. Forgiving what you'll never forget is REALLY HARD. It's something you walk out daily—you choose to forgive every day for your own peace of mind.

Here are some ways to practice forgiveness:

1. Practice mindfulness and feeling empathy. This will take work, trust me. Try to put yourself in the other person's shoes. Don't assume you know any motives to their actions and don't make it personal. Remove your ego and put yourself in their place. Feel empathy for them. When we see someone as a broken human versus someone who hurt us, it changes our heart.

2. Write or type a forgiveness letter. Let out all the things you forgive them for. You never have to give it to them if you don't want to. Again, forgiveness is for YOU. Feel that sweet release when you've done the deep work of writing this letter. Burn it up and remember to not pick those things back up again. Release the person for the damage they caused. Release yourself from the prison of bitterness.

SCRIPTURE REFLECTION:

"Bear with each other and forgive one another if any of you has a grievance against someone. Forgive as the Lord forgave you."

— Col 3:13 NIV

"Forgive others, not because they deserve forgiveness, but because you deserve peace."

— Jonathan Lockwood Huie

CHAPTER 6

A Change of Heart

THIS IS GOING TO happen a thousand times before you land on your feet. It's perfectly okay to change your mind and heart. As time progresses and you work on healing and growing, your perspective will change. You'll see things as they truly are and not how you thought they were. Emotions are the flashing red lights, warning us something is going on, but they are not the decision makers in your life. Once the dust settles, you can finally see the complete picture.

I want you to feel comfortable and safe in this part of the process. If you're still in love with your spouse and you want to fight for your marriage, do it. You might get a bit of backlash from family and friends, mainly because they are trying to protect you. Regardless, it's still okay to reconsider. It's still okay to want to end your marriage one week and fight for it the next. It really is part of the journey of healing. Sometimes your partner might be the first one with the change of heart. That might be what you need to see. You need to see your spouse trying or putting in the effort to want to make this work. Maybe that's going to motivate you to try again.

This is YOUR marriage! You will either be all in or not or stuck in the messy middle where you're still deciding. Your commitment to your decision is all or nothing or it will NOT work. While you are processing, it's okay to go back and forth. That's normal. Evaluate what's happening—can you truly move forward? Can you forgive and build a healthy relationship? These are a few things you need to ask yourself. Then, we need to ask the same of our spouse. Every marriage counselor will tell you to set boundaries for your marriage. You need to know your limits and your non-negotiables, especially now. Most of us do not know what it really takes to have a thriving marriage. I know I didn't. It takes WORK! A lot of good, hard, CONSISTENT work.

Do Over

While I love the concept of a "do over," it simply does not exist in real life. We can't erase everything that has happened and do it over. When you know better, you'll do better. If you didn't know better, that's why you are where you are now. No one is blaming you for anything that has happened in the past. You now have a unique opportunity to take all this collateral damage and analyze it. Decide what parts were good and worth keeping. Find all the things that slowly destroyed your marriage and you as a person.

Remember those things not as painful reminders of failure but as powerful lessons on how to improve.

I've been thinking so clearly over the last three weeks, and it has been eye opening. We don't realize there are things we could have done better for ourselves and for our marriage. People are quick to pass judgment and point fingers, but what can you change about YOU? Me, I'm a fixer. I want to fix my husband. I want to take everything he's saying and then find him a twelve-step program to fix it. Well, turns out he doesn't appreciate that very much. He used the same tactic on me a few times, and I realized how freaking annoying that was. Whoops! Girl, there's always grace for the things we can acknowledge and change within ourselves.

Now is the time when you get to fix yourself. You get to do you over. If you're going to work things out with your spouse, who do you want to be in this marriage? How can you show up for your marriage meaningfully? What is something you've learned through this process so far that you can change and start implementing in your life? How can you set yourself up for success in this relationship? What do you want your marriage to look like a year from now? Five years? Twenty years?

I know what you're probably thinking—how did we go from a change of heart to all these introspective questions and analysis? These are necessary questions to examine our heart. Are we being led by our emotions again? Are we currently feeling lonely, hormonal, tired, and hungry? Believe it or not, these things affect us daily. Thinking and meditating on these things allows us to see where we are with navigating our mind, heart, and soul. You only get one chance to show up for life. If you get the very rare and distinct chance to redeem your marriage, show up prepared and ready for it. Realize that both of you will take baby steps to heal your marriage.

Sounding Boards

I love my friends! Some of them are as brutally honest as I am, and I appreciate it so much. You need people like that in your life! I had three friends say the same thing to me on the same day. They told me some version of, "Veronica, don't forget to acknowledge his effort and progress. It may not be what you need, but it's what he's starting with. Acknowledge it in your heart and mention that you noticed."

I thought it was interesting that they all advised the same things despite packaging it differently. If I only see what I want, I am harsh and can overlook any progress that is happening. It was a sting to my pride, but I couldn't be more thankful for their honesty.

I realize that I have a tendency in my marriage to hyper-focus on why I'm so hurt or disappointed that I can't acknowledge my spouse's progress. We all process things differently, and it will not look or even feel the way you think it should. If it's progress, it's PROGRESS. Give your spouse some credit and a little grace.

"Veronica, give him a break. He's trying." You need to get good with your internal monologue you have going on. If you want this marriage to work on a second run, you need to be talking yourself out of crazy and talking yourself into giving some credit and grace. Loving someone is a combination of brutal honesty and outrageous amounts of grace. Its giving someone the space to evolve and giving yourself the same space. Brutal Honesty & Outrageous Grace. It's BOTH! I've spent my entire life until now nailing the brutal honesty part, but I've never practiced outrageous grace.

In my desperate need to be and feel fully known by my husband, I've been brutally harsh with him. I've shown little to no grace toward him in almost every circumstance. My expectation of him was unattainable—not only for him, but for me as well. So many things have happened over the course of my life that have made me respond this way, perhaps it's some kind of defense mechanism. Some self-preserving behavior, I'm not sure. What I am sure of is this—I want to practice outrageous grace and know what that feels like within the context of healthy boundaries. I want to get there. I don't want my husband to feel that I'm not a safe space for him. How amazing would it feel if someone extended outrageous grace to you every day? I don't know how to do this, but I am committed to learning this. The great thing about this is, you should have outrageous grace with everyone because everyone you meet is going through something. Practicing grace will benefit not only your marriage but your entire life.

I want to drive this home—there are NO DO OVERS—but you do get to start again. We can't erase anything that has happened, but we can begin again. Expecting a "do over" sets us up for failure because you will bump up against feelings and scenarios that trigger things from the past. What you've experienced will never go away, however, the new and wiser version of you knows you have a choice to deal with YOUR triggers. Triggers are the indicators that there's still a wound there that needs to be healed. It's not time for Band-Aids. It's time to do the real hard work of healing yourself and this marriage. Your faith walk will be the most pivotal part of this process. As I mentioned previously, prayer is vital to your healing. Learn how to pray. C.S. Lewis has a book on prayer that you can pick up, or a simple Google search on prayer can point you in the right direction. Process your pain in a way that benefits you in the long run. Once you decide what you want, decide. Be done with your decision-making and commit to following through with your choices.

Prayer Changes Things

I would love to sit here and pretend that I did everything right in this waiting process. I would love to take credit for my change of heart and my husband's, but the truth is I did nothing but surrender it all to God. I let my people help me and, frequently, I asked them to hold my arms up. They prayed for me, my baby girl, and my husband. They looked at us as a collective unit and not as individuals, which meant the world to me. My wounded heart couldn't muster up the courage to pray, so they whispered prayers.

I'll be honest . . . I didn't want to pray for God to heal our marriage because what if He didn't? I didn't want God to change my husband because then I would feel forced to "make it work." I didn't ask for any of this to happen, and I didn't want to bear the responsibility necessary for healing. That's my raw honesty, but I'm so thankful and eternally grateful for friends who could pray for my marriage. I know if may seem impractical to you to pray, but maybe that's because it's complicated to understand the power it holds. Our words hold weight in this life, especially our prayers.

How do you explain the countless miracles that happen in people's lives? I'm not talking about marriages being restored. I'm talking about physical healings, the out-of-this-world inexplicable stuff. Someone somewhere was praying. We all know someone personally or a friend of a friend who has had something miraculous happen. I want to be careful with this subject because I don't want you to think that you simply pray and a miracle happens. It may or it may not. There are so many undefined miracles that can take place. In the long term, we may not know what they are. Either way, prayer will change you. I get smarter when I pray, growing in wisdom and insight that I didn't have before. I feel myself being more patient and empathic toward my husband. Even if he's not changing, I am. I encourage you to try it. It can't hurt anything, can it? It might change everything.

Cease Fire

I can't really pinpoint exactly what made me snap out of my attack mode. Maybe I grew tired of always trying to defend something. I have a lot of fight in me about anything I'm passionate about, but I don't want to fight anymore. I'm not saying I don't want to fight for my marriage. I don't want to fight the other side of this marriage. I'm tired of arguing and going in circles; I want some freaking answers! Solutions are incredibly difficult to come by when you're angry. You become blinded by it. Pain is a pair of sunglasses for you—you can't see without them.

Maybe this is where you're at right now. I didn't think I would ever get to this place where I don't want to beat his face until it's bloody. Sorry for that graphic visual, but that's how much rage my husband sent coursing through my veins. I couldn't stand to be in the same room with him, and now I want to hear about his day. WHO AM I? I get it—I'm there right now. Nothing has changed except for me. I've changed. The fight is over for me. I'm ready for an all-or-nothing marriage. I don't want to feel constantly at war with him.

I've said this many times in my marriage: "You can't hurt me without hurting yourself." I would almost chant this to him and never listen to the words myself. Now, I've never intentionally hurt my husband—wait . . . that's not true. I've said several hideous things on purpose. I've aimed for the jugular more times than necessary. I've felt badly about it but never apologized because it was the truth. It's both a character flaw and my biggest strength, which is typical of most people. Your biggest strength is usually your biggest flaw. I decided not to be that way anymore. Today, I called a ceasefire in my heart.

I will stop attacking my husband with my hurtful words. I will learn the art of processing silently and only bring solutions to the table for both of us. I'm a fixer, so I always find solutions for him. What about for us? The fruits of the spirit will be my focus. I don't want to live this life angry. I don't want to look back ten years from now and wish I would've stopped my full-fledged war sooner. I want to experience ridiculous grace—with him and myself.

This may not resonate with you, but I pray it does because you are essentially warring against yourself. You are married, and when you're married two become one. Perhaps that's why the fight feels so hard. You are fighting yourself. Ummm, I don't know about you, but that's a mic drop moment for me. A light bulb went off in my head. I've messed it all up so badly. I've been fighting against myself because I can't hurt him without hurting myself. Think about this for a few minutes. Reflect on your behavior and what you've said and done with this season. Are you proud of yourself? Can you think of anything you could've done better? My list is excruciatingly long. I've begged and pleaded for him to consider all the things I've said and never done it myself. What a hypocrite!

> *"The primary cause of unhappiness is never the situation but your thoughts about it."*
> — Eckhart Tolle

That will preach!

Cold Hard Truths

As I'm writing this, my fingers are ice cold. It's a frigid day in Nashville. Something triggered me today in a way that makes me want to scream and be a fire-breathing dragon. My blood is boiling because I thought there was hope on the horizon and here comes my husband's indecision again. Nothing makes me angry more than indecisiveness. Life is not as hard as we all make it. You only need to decide and then make choices that support your decision. It really is that simple. Don't complicate things by overthinking everything—you're going to fry your brain.

Is it hard to draw some conclusions? Yes, but do it and be done with it.

I want my marriage to work because I don't see this as an impossible situation. Did I feel it was at times? YES! I could only see my pain and not solutions. I could only see truth tainted by rage and anger, which is NOT truth. Every single relationship in your life is going to require HARD work! All of them! I don't know why there are people who think relationships are easy because they're not. Whether you are processing alone or together, every single human being does it. Stop prolonging the process and dragging it out into a drama saga.

The cold hard truth may be that you are willing to work things out and he does not. That may be the reality you live in, and that's okay. If he walks away, that's on him. I know that doesn't make it easier to live with, but it's on HIM. It is possible for you to have peace in your heart because you tried to give it your all. You did all the counseling and sessions necessary to see results. It is not possible to make people grow up. If I had a magic lamp and genie, I swear that my wish would be for him to grow up. You don't know what you don't know, and he doesn't know what he's capable of or what your marriage is capable of. He only sees his failure and the overall failure of this marriage.

My husband wants to blame all of this on my personality. I want to laugh out loud every time he says we are too different because internally I think, "THANK GOD!" Thank God we are different! Thank God that I can see potential and possibility where you see failure. Thank God that I will stretch, bend, break, and remake myself for the sake of growth. Thank God that someone endures the pounding waves of life and says, "I will not drown or give up. I'm going to get stronger and learn how to ride these waves." If this sounds like you in the relationship, THANK GOD! Let's enjoy a moment of absolute gratitude for all we are learning in this process. You are eradicating weakness and dominating your wretched flesh. Thank GOD!

Immaturity and ignorance will have people making excuses for things not to work, but it works if you want it to work. Do what's necessary for success. A lot of times that will not be pleasant but learn to compromise and do what's needed in the moment to maintain peace, achieve clarity, and move this relationship forward. Ask yourself what you want. Do you want this? What is the gut response? The gut response is your truth. My gut response says I know this will succeed with time and work. My rational response is F#$K him! I'm being transparent with you. I'm getting my emotions in check today because if I've decided that I want this to work, then I need to support my decisions with my choices. Choosing not to flip out because I'm angry supports my decision that I want this. Giving myself a timeout supports my decision that I want this to work. Not texting everything I think to defend or justify myself supports this marriage.

I always want to defend myself. I want to say why I'm the perfect spouse for him and how much I believe in love and all the girly things. Yet I realize how damaging it is to be in that state of mind. You don't need to convince someone to stay—please don't do it. Speak your truth and leave it at that. Don't beg. The last thing you want is for someone to come home because of pity or convenience. You 100% deserve more than that, and you can fight for that in your marriage. Don't lower your standards to make this work. In fact, do the opposite. Set a higher standard for you to love more, be more attentive, grow more, read more, and practice that ridiculous grace. Raise the BAR! You will grow and that's your win!

Chapter Six:
Things to Think About

Your thoughts chart the course for your life. What are you constantly thinking about or obsessing over? Are they positive thoughts? Are you rehearsing the worst-case scenario? What thoughts are on repeat in your head?

I'm asking because what's going on between your ears matters so much. Your thoughts will lie to you. They will often be gross exaggerations of the truth. Learning how to get a hold of them is CRITICAL.

Here's how I practice controlling my thoughts:

1. Replace every negative thought immediately with something positive. Force yourself to reframe your thoughts constantly.

2. Reframe every lie or every hurt point of view with an absolute truth. Example: "No one is ever going to love me again." Replace that with "I am worthy of love and respect, and I will be with someone who loves and respects me when I'm ready to receive."

SCRIPTURE REFLECTION:

"Take captive every thought and make it obedient to Christ."

— 2 Corinthians 10:5 (NIV)

"The happiness of your life depends on the quality of your thoughts."

— Anonymous

CHAPTER 7

Love Again

I DON'T KNOW IF I can love my spouse the way I used to. I don't know if I can love anyone without being terrified of living through this kind of pain again. Love requires so much of you. If you're doing it right, you are daily dying to self. That means you can't shield yourself. You can't fully love someone while you're trying to protect yourself from getting hurt. Love is an all-in experience, it's all or nothing. You can't be on guard and free at the same time.

This is where I find myself today, wondering if I can love him or anyone else again. As women, we spiral down this path because it's our nature to love and desire to be known and loved. It's completely normal—after this level of trauma, how could we possibly feel comfortable to love again? I honestly don't know how I could without God.

Half-Baked Love

When I sit and truly consider how much God loves me, everything in my life pales in comparison. If I take a trip down Memory Lane of moments and events when I felt God's love so tangibly—as if He were in front of me—it inspires me to love again.

Humanity's brokenness is heartbreaking. I can only relate within the context of life with my child, who I love with every fiber of my being. My soul explodes with love for her and simultaneously aches for her. It's an intense, inexplicable love—there is no comparison. I think about this often when I'm holding her in my arms, about to put her to sleep. I love her more than anyone on the planet, but I don't love her more than God loves her. That blows my mind! His love is pure and devoted. The love of God is always in pursuit of our hearts, always accepting of our frailty, and always available to comfort. We are God's children, so imagine the intention and unconditional love behind it. This is the love I should have for my spouse, but I'm not able to right now. Remember that your spouse is someone's child whose parents love them, sees their brokenness, yet loves them through their challenges. They will inspire you to try again.

My love is in pieces right now. My heart has deep, gaping wounds that need repair. While I want to love him like I'm supposed to and am called to, I can't in this moment. However, if I'm being honest, it's not that I can't. It's that I won't. Something happens when someone hurts you this badly—you stop actively loving. What I mean by actively is that love is a verb, love is expressed via actions There's a book on that too called *Love Does* by Bob Goff. In his book he explores the idea that love is more than just the picture-perfect romance. It's certainly not a Hallmark movie—it is instead being present and sacrificing for the greater good. If I want to go all in and have what I've referenced several times—the outrageous grace and the brutal truth of the undefined miracle—then I must DO SOMETHING with all of this. As much as it might not work or even bring about the results I want, this is my last attempt. The pursuit of holiness in marriage requires dying to yourself daily. We walk in covenant with another person—learning about them, loving them, and choosing them daily.

This is where I feel the greatest tension within myself. I know I love him because that's what I've chosen but showing that is excruciating right now. Everything in me wants to protect myself from further damage, but if I risk nothing, then I won't gain anything either. In this life, risk is always required! You can't have the marriage you're dreaming about without taking risks. I won't have anything I'm praying for without taking the risk involved. This is a partnership between you and God to figure out the steps and put your faith into action.

Can We Be Friends?

I've reached a pivotal moment where I can no longer discuss all the details of who hurt whom the most. I'm so tired and beyond drained of running over the scenarios in my head and having no resolution. There will never be a way to resolve this. It's something horrible that happened. This experience isn't fun; I don't like it and I never will. But I'm praying that it will serve a greater purpose for my life and my future. I truly believe that in acceptance lies peace. That doesn't mean agreement. It simply means accepting this happened, that this is your world now, and deciding what you are going to do with it.

You can't keep rehearsing everything that went wrong. You could, but why? I'm so done with that. I need solutions. When I told my husband this, he was insistent on trying to figure out what's wrong with me and why he needs to think if he can add certain things about my personality. That made me so angry! How dare he try to pick personality flaws to justify what he doesn't like, adding to him making his dreadful decisions! I'm still angry about that because it makes little sense to me. If you're trying to find solutions, don't start by picking on another person. Period. If you want your marriage to win, analyze yourself. Start finding things you could do better daily to show up for your life and your marriage.

It's so important for you to take responsibility for yourself in this. Find ways you can grow and bring solutions to the table, not more problems. Your relationship must go back to a fundamental step—friendship. Do you even like your spouse as a person? Can you be friends? Do I even like him as a person? Write down the things you do like about the person. It's so easy to find flaws. Be the one that finds the gold in someone else. Find something in that person that makes you want to fight for this marriage.

I may be delusional, but I still think I can be happy and healthy in my marriage. I'm fully aware of how much work and effort it's going to take, but that's every area of life. Everything worth having requires work. Don't buy into the lie that if it was meant to be, it would be easy. ALL relationships are effort and work. It requires one hundred percent of both people. You can't get anything out of a relationship you're not putting into it. Consider what you are putting into the current state of your relationship. If you are going through with your divorce, what are you putting into yourself right now?

If you don't think you can restart or be friends and you want to bow out, that's okay. You have every right to your choice. That's your decision; be comfortable with it as hard as it may seem. Sometimes divorce is the healthiest option after an affair. Don't feel bad—it's your life and you know what you can handle. I applaud you because getting a divorce is painful, but it also speaks to your courage and bravery. You're not afraid of what other people think and the pain of recovery hasn't kept you in an unhealthy situation. I also want to challenge you—have you truly given this your all? It takes time to sort through the pain your spouse caused. Trust me, I'm right there with you. I get it. It takes time to sort through all those emotions and breathe fresh air again.

I'm asking you to consider not giving up because it's painful or you're scared. If those are not your reasons for moving forward with a divorce, then get the divorce. I'm convinced I haven't tried everything I can yet. Since he confessed to his affair, I have put little effort into our relationship. I didn't know how to process or even deal with him. I'm hoping this book helps you a little in that regard, but you learn as you go. There are no cookie-cutter options. It's all about effort and what each party will bring to the table.

To start fresh, you must reestablish boundaries in this friendship, especially down to the basic human concept of respect. I don't know if you feel like I do, but I don't have respect for my husband. I'm actively working on correcting this, but respect and trust are concepts that are earned, not assumed. For me, it's all about the little things. If you say you're going to do something, do it. I don't care what it is. It can be the dumbest thing, but if you say you're going to do it and don't, I have no respect for you. That translates to other areas of your life.

I've realized I have never communicated how important it is to me for people to follow through. People can't correct things they don't know about it. I think being fair and hitting the restart requires realizing what didn't work the first time. If you're honest with yourself, you'll see the things that slowly destroyed the relationship. It's little things that add up to the massive destruction. What are those little things in your life? Were they or are they in your relationship right now? Are there some boundaries that can get put into place now to prevent it from happening again?

Think about the friends in your life. What do you like about them? I'm a very fortunate woman to have a lot of close friends. I thoroughly enjoy my friendships because I've done the work to build them solidly. Are they perfect friendships? No, but I know we have mutual respect and love for each other. So why can't I have that in my marriage? I can! I must choose to rebuild from the foundation up. That sounds like a daunting task, and maybe it is. But if I want this to work, I must rebuild this—correction; WE must rebuild this.

I feel like I missed the point of marriage the first time around. Everything was heavy on the responsibility side and there was zero fun in it. You already know how everything played out the first year of my marriage. How much fun did I really have? None, and I think that was a big part of the problem. Being an adult is often boring and overwhelming, but it's because that's what we make it. What if we choose to prioritize creating wonderful experiences and having fun with our spouse and family? I bet the dynamic of the relationship would change drastically. Fun erases nothing that happened in the past, but it's easier to process fun than all the trouble you're trying to find solutions for. Let's have fun again!

Easier Said Than Done

As with most things in life, being friends with someone who betrayed your trust and shattered your marriage is easier said than done. I think the reason it's so hard, aside from the obvious, is our attitude toward it. Humans are quite resilient, but we are simply not wired to forget trauma. Unless you suffer from amnesia, you'll always remember this betrayal. But it won't always hurt this much. That's my goal—for it not to always hurt this much. I want to laugh again with my husband and be silly, maybe even have regular sex. I'm reaching for the stars in this, and why shouldn't I?

Life is so short and rarely do we find ourselves in the position to try again with better intentions. If the opportunity presents itself, take it. You must go all in and hold nothing back from this restart. Some people think restarts void everything that has already happened, but it doesn't. There must be so much grace for both people here. You need grace from your spouse because this trauma will not heal so easily, and he/she needs grace from you. You really can't keep hanging things over their head and vice versa. Also have grace for yourself. There will be days when you're going to be bumping up against all the feelings. Take a deep breath and have grace for yourself.

I mentioned earlier that you need to be a solution-oriented partner. Life and marriage are not as hard as we make it sometimes. We make it hard with our pride, our selfishness, our bitterness, and our pain. All these things cloud our judgment and prevent us from seeking truth and solutions. I also feel it's important to mention that this will not work if you are waiting for the other person to make the first move. I know we are the ones who experienced hurt and betrayal and it doesn't seem fair, but life isn't about fair. You need to remove that from your brain. How do you want the outcome to look? If you want to reconcile this marriage, then you need to show up in your best version every day, not when they do something nice for you.

I'm saying this to myself every day because it is a challenge. I still want vengeance! You and I are both human. Our hearts long for redemption, but I truly believe it will come with time. I believe we can still live our best days even in the middle of this. We can still have purpose and intention in our hearts regardless of what's coming at you. You must decide and let every choice you make support your decision. I know that's a repeat line because it's so important! Bring 100% of you to the table every day. Show up for yourself, your marriage, your kids, and your career. Decide that no matter what, you are going to show up without excuses. That's what it's going to take to get out of this place.

The Tension is Real

I am not immune to the pain anyone would feel having lived and experienced this. There are many days that I still can't believe this is my life, and this is the story I get to tell. I didn't choose any of this. Maybe I did with the sum of all my choices. What I know is that I feel this incredible tension within me even now. I'm trying to focus on gratitude, to say positive affirmations, to dream and set goals.

Lately, I've been a little depressed. My husband is back in the house, and I don't know how to function again. I had my life down to a science and a routine where I only needed myself. I could manage my growing toddler and the chaos that often brings on top of my full-time job and other demands of life as a boss. This week, I feel like I'm failing all over again. Why is that? He's been gone for three months and it's as if the entire house is adjusting to his presence again.

There's a lot of uncertainty here because I can't control him or how he feels. I wish I could fast forward and see a glimpse of what the future would look like, but no such thing exists. Instead, I feel stuck and perhaps slowly becoming overwhelmed with a million what ifs. What if he cheats on me again? What if this second chance is the same or worse than the first go around? What if he's not really going to work on his own personal growth and change? What If I'm never going to have the marriage I want with him? It's these thoughts bouncing around in my head that have ruined my sleep, caused me to grind my teeth at night from stress, and have me feeling drained. My emotions are affecting so much of my life right now, even the areas I don't talk about.

I don't really want to talk to anyone about this because I'm afraid they will only confirm what I'm feeling. I feel judged if I decide to work it out. Others will judge me if I decide to walk away. Everywhere in this is someone else's opinion. Eleanor Roosevelt said it best: "What other people think of me is none of my business." So true! It takes courage to end your marriage, but don't for a second think it doesn't take courage to stay. It takes some serious determination, a lot of faith, and a lot of tears.

Courage Above All Else

The people who have never found themselves in this exact situation are usually the first to judge. I know I was when I heard about it happening to other people. I made my vows that I would never put up with blah blah blah . . . etc. We have all done that from time to time, but it's not until we live that scenario that we realize we don't know what we're going to do. Sure, it's easy to say, "Well, if my husband ever cheated on me, I would leave him immediately and file for a divorce." I wouldn't even think about it, but most likely it will not happen.

Your marriage is sacred, and you will feel compelled to make it work—maybe not forever, but for a season. What you didn't know when making judgmental statements was that marriage takes courage. It takes courage to walk away, and I would dare say it might take even more to stay after someone has hurt you so badly. Outsiders may not acknowledge this, so I will. It will damn near take all the courage and strength you have to make it through this, regardless of what you decide.

Courage means you are doing this scared. You don't have all the answers and you do not know what in the world this is going to look like, but you are pressing forward. I don't believe there's a one-size fits all answer for dealing with an affair. I don't think most people will counsel you correctly. You will ultimately navigate this alone, and that's okay. You will discover strength and courage you never thought possible. It is extremely rewarding to survive something on your own. I have amazing friends/family who encourage me and pray over my marriage, but we do the hard work alone. No one is there to wipe your tears except your pillow but know that God is keeping track of them and collecting them (Psalms 56:8. NLT). YOU are exactly what you need right now. You need ALL of you to rise from the ashes and declare yourself a warrior, because you are one.

Boundaries

I'm sure you have a lot of well-meaning people in your life who love you. We can't live without them and sometimes we can't live with them. These are the overly opinionated people who are currently bashing your decision to start again and to give your marriage a second chance. I know they mean well; you know they mean well too, but it does nothing to diminish the sting.

I'm sure your closest friends or family members are all dealing with their own grief and anger from your betrayal, but they really need to keep that in perspective. It's your life, not theirs. You are the one who suffered this egregious act and having them bash you and demean you is not a morale boost. I wish so badly I could tell that you will feel

100% supported, but you won't. People closest to you will hold a lot of weight in your world and you will have to be so careful who you are listening to.

I have had a lot of very harsh words spoken to me in this season, and I've taken it all with a grain of salt. Know that people are processing all this too. Some will process better than others. Some will separate their emotions from what you need to feel supported. Others will not, and that's okay. You must guard yourself and place boundaries on the people you feel are attacking and demeaning your decisions. It's healthy and ok to do that. Establishing solid boundaries is healthy. Truthfully, they are critical right now.

Now to address this from the perspective of a mother or parent. I never want to hear a story like this coming out of my daughter's mouth. I never want her to be in this position or feel this level of pain, ever. As her mother, it would be beyond devastating to watch her go through this, so I understand where my mother is coming from. She's furious, and rightfully so. I get it. No one wants to see his or her kids hurt. She needs to process her pain and her anger as well. When a person doesn't do this, they say things that are hurtful to the person already hurting.

Don't feel the need to defend your decisions or actions. Be aware that they are hurting too and give them some grace. I know my mother isn't trying to hurt me; she's equally scared and worried for me, which I appreciate. Try to understand where they are coming from, especially a parent. They are trying to protect their child. I know that some things they say will hurt like hell and feel like they are confirming all your biggest fears, but you have a choice in how you respond. You've already been through enough and if you need to take some space to reestablish boundaries, do so.

 I will admit that I have been avoiding conversations about my marriage like the plague. I don't want to talk about it with my mom. If I'm having a bad day, all my venting will spill out and adds fuel to her fire against my husband. I want peace. While I recognize it will take time for everyone to feel okay together, I am committed to that process. This healing time is sacred, whether you've decided to stay or go. It's a unique time for you to heal and grow. We've had enough toxic things happen. I want to clear the air and have peace in my heart and mind again, and I will protect that at all costs. You should protect your peace, too.

Chapter Seven: Things to Think About

Everyone has boundaries. It takes a very long time to figure out why I am upset about something until I realize it is because someone or something has violated a boundary. Fair warning on this—when you hold the line on your boundary, it's going to upset people that were used to violating it. HOLD THE LINE. You need to identify what the boundary is for you.

Here's an example of one of mine—I need alone time. If I don't get enough alone time, I get very cranky. I recharge best in solitude. I can't be "on" all the time and in social settings, my timer is done in about thirty mins. I'm tapped out and want to go home and sleep.

I know it's not the same for everyone, but for me it's a lot. This is something that most people don't understand about me, so it comes across as rude or uninterested. In those situations, I'm tapped out. I need to be alone. This is equally my fault, too. I must honor what I need and not expect someone to respect a boundary I can't hold. Now it's time to identify some boundaries for yourself.

Here's an exercise for you to try this week:

1. Make a list of your boundaries. Evaluate how you enforce them or how you've not held the boundary for yourself.

2. What can you do to help you make sure you're honoring yourself and what you need right now?

SCRIPTURE REFLECTION:

"Above all else, guard your heart, for everything you do flows from it."

— Proverbs 4:23-26 (NIV)

"I set boundaries not to offend you, but to respect myself."

— Unknown

CHAPTER 8

A Hug A Day

OH, THE WORLD OF love languages! How wonderfully complex they are . . . or are they? I never realized how important love languages were until I got married. We were both aware of what they were, but it never seemed to click why it was important until now. My love languages are Quality Time and Physical Touch in a tie. Words of Affirmation and Acts of Service are my husband's. Did you notice something here? We don't have any love languages in common. This is NORMAL AND COMMON. It has never been clearer than in this rebuilding phase of our marriage.

I'm such a quality time and physical touch person. Give me all the snuggles. I feel loved best when someone is spending time with me one-on-one. I also don't feel loved when someone has spare time and spends it doing something else without me. This has been a major issue in our relationship. I've always felt like an option and never a priority. The physical touch in this relationship is non-existent. It's no wonder I've been so miserable, practically begging to be loved. He didn't love me the way I needed, according to how I receive love. Also, admittedly, vice versa.

How could I say anything affirming when I felt like I was drowning in pain and so neglected? I felt constantly rejected by him based on how I need love. My acts of service were doing laundry and cooking, which were well received, but words are a big deal to him. I am brutally honest and that comes across as not being supportive or understanding. I get that, even though it was and is far from my intention. He shuts down when he isn't being affirmed, and I give love the way I need to receive it.

Does that make it right? NO! Does it make it wrong? NO! It's a matter of two people committing to learn how to love the other person in the way they best receive love. I guess the reason I feel like I'm failing here is because most everyone in my life has the same love language I do. My husband is my polar opposite. Does it mean it will never work? No. It means we will have challenges and need to be intentional about addressing them. It also means we must speak up and help the other person love you the way you need it.

Think of the love you need as a bank account. When someone loves you well, the way you receive it, you're getting deposits made. Conversely, when someone doesn't love you well in the way you receive love, you're getting withdrawals. I'm in a straight up negative bank account with a million overdraft fees. No exaggeration here. What

I've recently realized is that he is too. Love will not function in negative accounts. Will you always have a fat love bank account? Maybe not, but it should at least be a goal to strive for.

So, what's next? I suppose we must address these severely negative love bank accounts. What would it take to fix this? I believe the answer is incredibly simple. CONSISTENCY. If you want your bank account to grow, you need to make daily deposits into it. Remember, you are already in the red, so it's going to take some time for you to clear that account up of all the negatives. There may be days when you don't care enough to try. I'm there a lot of days. I feel like a hormonal roller coaster; not that it's an excuse, but it's real to me. Pursuit takes discipline and consistency and if I'm being honest, I've sucked in both areas lately.

I haven't loved my husband in the way he needed to be loved. That is a very hard pill to swallow for me because I pride myself on being an exceptional lover of people. It sounds silly for me to say that, but it's true. I love LOVE my people! If you are in my circle or my close friends, you are like family to me, and I deeply love you. I figured loving my husband would never be this difficult, but it is sometimes. I'm a grumpy old lady who's so set on her ways that she doesn't even see she's wrong. Lately, I've had to deal with that lady in the mirror. She needs to allow light into the dark places she is trying to keep to herself. I must tell her to listen more than she speaks and really try to hear what he's saying. It has not been easy because this is how I am, but I will not use that as an excuse to not grow or change.

We have choices in life and how you choose to love others is one of them. Love is 100% pursuit even when you don't want to. Humanity has gotten so far off center in how we love people. We love people from a place of interest and convenience. Yep! I said it! We all love people either from interest or convenience. If they serve a certain purpose in your life, great! Once they no longer serve you, you're done. I've done this—not intentionally, but it's interesting to examine past relationships and get down to the core of why they no longer exist. It may surprise you to find that you fall into one of these two categories.

Here's the thing—love is everything but convenient. Growing up and loving someone who has shattered your heart is not convenient. It's not convenient to forgive someone, although it is entirely beneficial to you. And it's certainly not convenient to swallow your pride and learn how to love someone in the way they need to be loved. None of it is convenient, but all of it is necessary to build a beautiful relationship. The marriage you always dreamed of will never be convenient. The relationships you've always wanted will not be convenient. Love is a choice in the face of fear and pain. It really is pushing yourself to love better, to be more gracious, and to practice outrageous grace.

Now, with all that being said, let's revisit the negative bank accounts. Right now, I am trying to have grace with my husband. I realize we must re-adjust to him not living here for three months and now, boom! We are a family again with all the awkwardness and weird vibes. I know it's expected and normal, but that doesn't mean it doesn't bother me. It does so much, and again I question why this is my life. Why isn't my life a Hallmark channel movie specifically with Ryan Paevey falling madly in love with me? Haha! On a serious note, it's a constant internal struggle to push past these expectations I have and face the reality I'm currently living.

The easiest way to become disappointed is to have unmet expectations or expectations that are not communicated. I have been communicating more of my annoyances and that I'm disappointed rather than explaining why that is. For example, since my love languages are quality time and physical touch, I want a hug every day and a kiss at least. This is the bare minimum plan. It pains me that sometimes I must tell my husband to give me a hug or a kiss. I am embarrassed and feel ashamed, but it's ridiculous for me to feel that way, especially if that's what I need. It's an extremely raw and vulnerable place for me, considering all the times he has rejected me. Yet here I am again, because love doesn't quit and requires putting yourself in a position to be vulnerable.

When I wrote the title of this chapter, I wrote it angrily. I was angry that I was getting a hug a day, and it felt like a reward for "good behavior." Now that some of my anger has settled, I realize that all of this is equally awkward for him, too. It's easy to only consider your emotions in this season. For obvious reasons, you feel yours are more valid, but that's not true. Both of your feelings and emotions are valid! Does that mean you need to spew them out at each other every day? Heck no! Practice silence sometimes—not the silent treatment, but quiet your feelings until you've sorted them out.

There are minor victories in this, and you need to train your heart and mind to see them. I'm bad at this. I have so many expectations and I'm trying to adjust them, communicate them, and reevaluate some others. The hard work in marriage is what you BOTH refuse to see and acknowledge, whether good or bad. The areas you BOTH refuse to compromise again, good or bad. All of it falls back on both of you. However, I am a huge advocate for taking personal responsibility and fully owning your part in this. No one is a mind reader. I know many people in this position won't agree with this last paragraph. I know you won't because I didn't for a very long time. I used to think marriage would work or not. Never did I realize it would take constant adjustments, and mostly being aware of your own expectations. Marriage requires CONSTANT GROWTH & ADJUSTMENTS. This little nugget will serve and benefit all your relationships, evaluate your expectations.

Limiting Beliefs

I'm sure this concept isn't new to anyone, but in case it is, let me explain. A limiting belief is a belief that you acquire because of an incorrect conclusion. If this marriage fails, I could develop a limiting belief that marriages fail or that I am not fit for marriage. Both are incorrect and not true and based on my experience and how I process it. It's so easy to develop a lot of limiting beliefs about your marriage, especially after having survived an affair. Another limiting belief could be that it's pointless to try because he'll do it again.

I used to struggle with this thought daily because my fear wanted to keep me in a place of bondage and not freedom. The reality is it could happen again. I pray to God it doesn't, but it's not outside of the realm of possibility. I can't, however, make that the reason I don't try or don't give my all to this marriage. If I've decided to stay and work it out, then I owe it to myself foremost to become a whole person, to work on myself, and work on my relationship with my husband. If you're going to surrender to fear, you might as well give up now. There's no room for fear when you must rebuild something.

Did trust magically reappear? HELL NO! If I'm being honest, this is the hardest part. How do I know I can trust him? I don't always know. Most days I rely heavily on my intuition and if I feel something is off, I ask him. Yet again, trust is a choice. I one million percent believe it must be earned, no question. What I'm saying is that our fear can distort our judgment of what's true or not. Our fear can have us doubtful of normal things. I've taken a step back and asked myself why I'm not trusting in specific moments. Is it because this looks like another moment in the past? Is it because I'm PMSing and feeling all kinds of anxiety? Am I tired? Am I living in the past? What's in my heart right now that I must address?

The biggest takeaway from this process has been looking at myself first. No one likes to admit that they are wrong, no one. People don't like to look in the mirror and see a broken piece. No one! Yet it is so necessary in our lives. It's so healthy to have these reflective times when we evaluate our hearts, minds, and our soul's conditions. I was angry about the hug a day. It made me feel unworthy and gross, and I had to come to terms with that being a lie I was choosing to believe. I am worthy of a hug and so much more! What my husband was choosing to do or not do to make me feel that way reflects what's going on in my heart. This is me owning up to my own feelings of self-worth and taking responsibility for them.

1,000 Sad Tears

I'm sad for a thousand different reasons, but I can't tell you which one hurts the most. All I know is that I carry a heavy wound within the recesses of my heart. I don't even know that time will heal them. What does it even mean to mourn something you've lost? I've lost time, experience, ideals, and expectations. I've lost so many things and daily I talked myself back into fighting for another day. It's all fine and dandy that I've made this work, but damn, the reality is excruciating. A lot of days I don't want to make it work. I want to make ME work.

I want to grab all the pieces still floating out there in space and put ME back together. This overwhelming sadness needs to go. I don't want to trust the process; I want the process to be over. I want to know a deep happiness, not this deep sadness. I can't even describe the heaviness that sits in the middle of my chest, but you know it too. Or you know someone who's living this, too. There is nothing harder than forgiving someone who deliberately hurt you, one who chose himself over everything without a care in the world. The struggle is SO real.

You're probably thinking, *What the hell? You were in such a good place a chapter ago.* That chapter was months ago and a lot of life happens in a couple of months. This journey is going to be up and down and all over the place. It's going to have mountaintops and deep dark valleys. It's going to be all the things, hopefully not all at the same time. This month, it's a dark valley and I don't see the light at the end of the tunnel. I'm angry again that I'm here. He did what he did, and I am angry that this is my life. I'm angry that I don't feel like I have a family. It's now my daughter and me.

His presence and his absence feel the same to me. I hate that! I'm an overwhelmed, hard-working, loving momma. I'm killing myself for this "family." I'm doing all the things he refuses to do. I don't know how to respect someone like that. I don't know how to encourage someone that I truly feel is failing. Even worse is that I don't care to encourage him. I don't want to! He doesn't have my back, but I want to feel that. I have my back. It pains me to say this because this is so far from the life I thought we would live.

My world genuinely functions better without him in it. My house feels at peace, I sleep better, and my daughter goes to bed easier. I'm a better mom and human when he's not around. What is that, though? I think it's easy for us to take breaks and look for escapes, especially when we are hurting so much. Nevertheless, it's the truth. He got back after being gone five days and they were the best five days I've had in a long time. I spent so much quality happy time with my daughter. I went to sleep at a decent hour or watched the Hallmark channel in peace. I had space to live and be happy. Lately, I feel like I'm suffocating when he's home. He throws the entire schedule off. I don't know what it is about his energy, but it literally annoys the crap out of me.

I was in the best mood until he got home. Next day, I woke up in the worst mood, beyond exhausted and hateful. I hate who I am when he's around. There's so much angst. He asked me if I missed him while he was gone. I had nothing to say. I didn't miss him. I gave him a blank stare. I've grown accustomed to doing and living on my own. Am I at an impasse? I really don't know. What I know is that this is all so freaking hard. I'm at the point where a divorce sounds as good as a delicious cookies and cream sundae with hot fudge and whip cream on top.

Then I get this outstanding realization that all of this is "normal." By normal, I do not mean that it's right or that it's the way it should be. I mean that more people than not are in this same boat. They are frustrated, miserable, and hurting because of a seemingly hopeless marriage. I hope you find some comfort in knowing you're not alone. You are not the only person having to go through this level of hell and hard. Does that make it any easier? Hell no, but at least you're in good company.

It was a long time before I told anyone what I was going through. There were a lot of conflicting emotions there. Shame was a major player. The other thing that kept me from sharing was I didn't want to hear someone else's sob story. I didn't want to see someone who's been through it and came out better. I felt it was setting me up for false hope. That couldn't be my story because my husband is too immature and too selfish. We compare ourselves to other people for random good things, but did you realize you compare your battle scars, too?

A struggling marriage is not a joke and when your marriage is struggling, you cannot imagine someone else's pain level. I had this discovery a while ago—we all get dealt our own personal brand of hard. We experience hurt, but we certainly do not all hurt the same and over the same things. Comparing your wounds will do nothing to make you feel better about yourself. You know what will, though? Sharing what you've learned! Share what gave you hope, what gave you strength, books, sermons, podcasts. Share the things that gave you a shimmer of hope to try again. This is what we need to hear! It's what I need to hear, so I try my best to be that to someone else who's struggling.

Wave after Wave

Grief is a malicious spirit. One day you're fine and then next day you're drowning again. I have so much fear surrounding my future. Will I ever love again? Will I ever trust someone again? If I'm being entirely honest, my biggest fear is that this will never not hurt this much. I can work myself up into full-blown hyperventilating sobs if I let my thoughts linger long enough. Sometimes I hate myself for it, other times I feel like it's releasing emotional constipation. I've become very good at glazing it over, putting on some sweet sugary coating to hide the bitterness.

It's all a process and a necessary part of it. I must keep reminding myself that even though I don't know how this ultimately will work out, I must trust that it's for the best. Our lives are teaching us something. Grief is showing me my resilience. Grief is a frigid winter storm. It's being stuck in those elements unprepared; the winds blowing so hard and freezing against your body and you're praying you make it. Your body is doing all the labor to withstand dying alone in this storm. Grief feels like you're dying. I feel like I'm dying some days. I want to give up and give in to my pain, but there is no victory in surrender.

It's Game Time

I don't know what it is about me that is so damn stubborn. I want to look pain in the eyeballs and tell it to F off.

I've tossed the idea of getting divorced back and forth for months. I list out all the pros and cons. I think, and then I think again; it's exhausting. Then it hit me. My problem wasn't fear or grief. It was that I didn't decide. Sure, I said I was fighting for my marriage, but what was I fighting for? Someone who displayed the highest level of betrayal and disrespect. Um, yeah, I think I'll pass. Truth be told, I was fighting for my daughter to have her father in her life. I can't control that and me staying has been me trying to control that.

Growing up in a divorced home, I remember all the uncomfortable moments. I never wanted that for my kid and having to live this is breaking me down. But I can't be responsible or in control of their (her and her dad) relationship. I can only be responsible for mine with her. The more I thought about it, the decision became clearer—I had already mentally checked out. My heart was too wounded to feel anything except hatred and disgust for him. My fight was misguided and not genuine. I was trying to control him and in fear that he would abandon her. I couldn't look into my daughter's eyes and tell her she was worthy of love, respect, admiration, and honor and withhold those standards in my own life. The last thing I would want is for her to settle because she's scared. Which meant I had to be very, VERY brave and call it. I'm filing for a divorce.

I would be lying if I told you that conversation went well. It didn't. Everyone has this ridiculous idea that their spouse will suddenly know how to be an adult. It's laughable, really. I don't know why I expected it to go smoothly. It turned into an all-out war. My emotions were out of control. I want to make him pay for all the shit he's put me through, but no amount of verbal assault or tears will change anything. I still tried (shameful moment). The level of frustration that your life is completely f*cked? Sorry, but there's no other word for it. Everything you hoped for, wished for, and thought you attained is gone. Ripped away from you and left like roadkill. That's what I feel. I had to pull the trigger or continue living in a vicious cycle of torture.

Chapter Eight:
Things to Think About

Let's talk about those limiting beliefs. I didn't realize I had so many until going through this. What a truly eye-opening experience! If you're anything like me, you've realized maybe you wouldn't even be where you are now had you thought a little differently about yourself. OUCH! That's how I feel. Who the hell was I when I met my ex and why did I think I didn't deserve everything I said I wanted? Why did I settle for this? Why am I still settling for this?

Be honest with yourself and evaluate the limiting beliefs that got you here and still have you here.

And now, for a little exercise:

1. Identify as many limiting beliefs as you can about yourself. Dig deep and trace them back to their origins. Evaluate how they have affected your life.

2. Pick one of those limiting beliefs each week or month or however long it takes and reframe it. Tell yourself a new truth DAILY to train your brain to think differently.

> *"If you accept a limiting belief, then it will become a truth for you."*
>
> — Louise Hay

CHAPTER 9

Filing Day

FILING FOR DIVORCE WAS the hardest decision I've ever made in my life. When I filed, I felt so much more confident than I have ever felt before. I didn't feel like the champion at the end of a long battle. I felt defeated but picked myself off the floor for another round in the ring. I had every emotion and walked into that courthouse with fear and trembling. I felt embarrassed, brave, stupid, shame . . . a lot of random different things. When it was done, I felt peace.

I sat in my car and cried before driving back to work. I knew I made a hard decision, one that would hurt for a long time but would ultimately bring me peace and a better life. There are so many times when we are so afraid of the pain that we let it keep us stuck in a place we don't want to be. We let our fear of pain keep us from experiencing more. Life is painful, too painful sometimes, but pain will teach you so much if you sit with it. You must choose the hard path for the better good. I'm not saying the hard path is divorce. Maybe for you, the hard path is staying in your marriage. Don't let the pain or the fear of pain keep you stuck. You need to push through it.

The power of choice is such a gift. Think about it—you get to decide what you do. It's a gift that is so under appreciated. When I filed for divorce, I felt released from my chains. Finally, I could do something with this mess, and I did. It empowered me to write this book. I'm choosing to make a better life for myself and daughter by pursing my dreams and being the example I want her to see. I want her to know that she can always choose to change directions. You don't have to keep walking the same road because you've been on it for a while. This applies to every area of your life. Sometimes you must be brave enough to start again. See where your courage will lead you.

Take Time to Heal

I wish healing was an overnight process, I really do, but it takes time. You can't rush it. It's like a good marinade—you must let it sit. Allow yourself the time and energy to feel things and process them. Unfortunately, that is extremely difficult with a toddler. All of me is going to her and my job and I'm feeling like I'm about to crack. I want to be the best version of myself for her, but my well is running dry and depleted. I need a break, but life doesn't give you a break. Being a single mom affords you NO BREAKS. It's you all the time—you cook, you clean, you walk the dog, take out the trash, deal with the tantrums, wipe the tears, change the diapers, pick up the messes, barely shower, and somehow in all of that I'm supposed to heal? How? Did I mention my child is refusing to sleep at night? Fun times!

I must do better, but I'm beyond tired—mentally, physically, and emotionally. The worst part is I think my daughter knows. Ugh! Nothing breaks your heart more than seeing your kid struggle or sad. I need a breakthrough in my life, a consistent routine to get back into some sort of rhythm. I need a miracle. Ha! Back to needing that undefined miracle in my life. I've been furious with God lately. I am exactly like a toddler throwing a tantrum with God right now. If my kid doesn't sleep, I'm pissed at God. If my dog is barking, I'm pissed at God. Too much traffic? it's God's fault. It sounds ridiculous when I type that out, but it's real.

I guess I'm so frustrated that He can do anything but doesn't. My entire life could change in an instant for the better, heck, for the best, and it's not happening. Instead, I find myself in situation after situation, one harder than the next. I need someone to blame and God, you're it right now! I know I'm not the only one in this boat. You can only look up and shake your fists at God when you are in this place. You know what? It's okay! God can handle the rage and anger we feel. He can handle my disappointment. I don't think God is sitting up there angry at me and saying, "Nope, you will struggle forever now." He's not. It's my brokenness telling me that.

I think that once you get to the place where everything is God's fault, it's time for a timeout. You are thinking and feeling way too much! There is so much value in learning to sit down and process. Meditate, pray, breathe. It's easy to spiral when you're this angry. It's human nature to want to negate responsibility. Yes, I said responsibility, because ultimately, we can't control what happens, but we are responsible for our response to it. Sound repetitive yet? We have the power to choose our response. We can choose to heal.

So, what did I do? I cried, duh! Yes, I cried a lot, but then I felt better. I wrote down some things I wanted to see happen in my future, things I could work towards and achieve. I got a game plan together. You will 100% drown if you stay angry! It will only grow if you continue to feed it, so instead you need to focus on something positive. Your anger will bleed into every area of your life, EVERY AREA! It happens to many people, and I've slipped into it myself. I refuse to be this angry. I choose to heal from all of this.

Life is not for the faint of heart. Muster up the courage to keep it moving. Start again, build again, find a dream, choose a path, and be brave! Whatever that looks like for you, do it! You don't have time to sit and wait until you're not angry anymore. Don't wait for another person to choose you or pick you; YOU PICK YOU! If you are being treated as an option, then it's time to make yourself the priority! That doesn't mean abandon your marriage. It means fix yourself! When you are better, your marriage will be better! If you decide to divorce, then it's 100% about you now. Do better! Make better choices! Do things that will line up with your preferred future! Absolutely every decision you make is adding up to your future life, so choose wisely!

Gratitude

You can choose to stay angry, and you have the right to, but what if you chose gratitude instead? What if you changed your perspective and see what it's teaching you? Pain and experience are the best teachers! Instead of seeing yourself as the victim, see yourself as a special person who gets to live this out and learn, grow, and flourish from this disaster. I'm choosing to believe that my best days are ahead. My divorce won't be collateral damage and somehow everything will work out for my good. How that plays out is not entirely up to me, but I can choose to be grateful. Gratitude keeps you grounded and focused on good things. It's a posture of the heart and keeps things in perspective—your life is not that bad. You will always have something to be grateful for.

I really want to take some time to focus on gratitude mainly because it's extremely difficult for me most days. I have somehow turned into a complainer; I know, so annoying. I hear myself go on and on about everything going wrong, and he's this or that, and then this happened, and when I'm finished talking, I'm like, OMG who was that?! Focusing on things I'm grateful for shuts that down. What I'm carrying is heavy. It's constantly weighing on my heart and mind. I do a good job pushing forward, but my complaining and negative self-talk remind me that I'm not healed yet.

It's okay that I'm not healed yet. There's a lot to process, but I still want to be a grateful for my life and this season. We went to Disney one April as a family. I remember walking around Disney and seeing all these happy families enjoying the magic and wonder. I didn't have that; I don't have that, and I was almost in a puddle of tears until I realized what I have. What I have is an incredibly intelligent beautiful daughter, she has a father who loves her, and she loves him. We shared a trip that, regardless of how awkward, was a first-time event for our family. These are the trips you envision of having when you have a family and it happened for us.

I could've ruined the entire Disney vacation by focusing on what I didn't have, but how many people wish they had the money to go to Disney? How many kids wish they knew their dad or mom? I know that's taking it to the extreme, but it adds perspective. Nothing is going to be perfect, and I must choose to be grateful with what is in my hands now. I think we only got one family picture and honestly, I will cherish it. In that one picture, we felt like a family and, at the very least, we look like a happy one. It's something my daughter will have forever and I'm grateful for that.

Burn the Ships

The universe has waged a full-fledged assault on my sanity lately. Maybe it's hormones, who knows? I'm in a pressure cooker and about to explode out of it. Everything seems like it's falling apart—literally everything. My job should get a little less stressful in theory and it's increasing exponentially. Nothing I do is good enough, and I'm beyond exhausted of the toxic work culture. I'm single mommying it BIG time as fall tour season has started, and I am burnt out. I've lost ten pounds in two weeks from stress alone.

My body hates me right now as fall pollen is in all its glory in Nashville. I can't breathe, literally. I went to the

ER because I couldn't take it anymore. My anxiety is at an all-time high and my patience with the universe at an all-time low. I'm getting ugly on the inside. I feel it. Do you recognize when you're getting ugly? Everything bothering you lately? Being short and abrasive? Overly emotional or emotionally numb? Anybody there yet too? Whew, it's time for a break! Then, as I'm dealing with all this havoc inside of me and around me, my one constant, my amazing nanny, puts in her notice. It's enough for me to have a melt down at work.

What do I do? I say f*ck it. Burn the ships! Let the pieces fall where they may! Everything is coming to a stop, as if the universe is saying LET IT ALL GO! Imagine me as Elsa turning the world into my own icy castle. Lucky for her, she doesn't have to deal with anyone, and she can run away. I cannot. In all seriousness, everything came to a head in my life. My job was causing most of my anxiety and stress. My stress and anxiety were rubbing off on my baby and I can't have that. I only get one opportunity a day to be the best me and lately I'm missing it BIG TIME.

I'm not saying follow in my ridiculous footsteps of quitting your job. What I am saying is you can't be all things to all people. You are not Jesus. You need to realign your priorities and set some healthy boundaries in your life. My stuff was all over the place and because of it, my stress and anxiety were at an all-time high. It's okay to let a few people or commitments go if it means you're happy. I was doing way too much for way too long, and I think it became my escape. Yet ultimately, it all caught up with me. Here I am, having this massive bonfire over my life. BURNING the ships!

Speaking of bonfires, how amazing is fall, minus the pollen? You know, I've never been a huge fan of it, but this year I am. I love football season something fierce, but more than that, I feel hope in the air. As I see the leaves hit the ground and blow around, I can't help thinking about all the pieces of my life that feel like they are blowing in the wind. It's terrifying and freeing. New seasons require blank slates. I've never realized how much life imitates seasons. Summer is my jam, and I'm wanting a summer season in my life. I am bracing myself because "WINTER IS COMING!"

What is Winter?

Winter is barren, brutally cold, and blank. When I close my eyes and think of winter, I see a forest of trees covered in snow, the bark of trees being this grayish white color, and the ground covered in clean snow. It's beautiful and peaceful, but bare. My winter is coming when everything is going to be new but blank. I will get to rebuild my life with the people, the job, the happy I want in it. It's such a deeply peaceful thought for me. I know that the blank slate can seem overwhelming and scary, but what if it's all that and something crazy beautiful?

I'm desperately ready for a win in my life. I'm no longer scared of the what ifs. You know what's going to happen? I'm going to move forward, make better choices for myself and my daughter and pursue being the best version of myself. I'm going to grow, take risks, and keep pushing. I will introduce colors in the blank snow. It's my life and winter has the potential to be so breathtakingly beautiful but, alas, I can't deny the level of pain that will come with it.

Winter is barren because life becomes dormant, sometimes withering away. My marriage was dormant, and I feel parts of me were dormant as well. The fairy tale ending with a knight in shining armor, dead. The perfect little family that stays together, dead. Being the best wife and having an adoring husband, very dead. Things must die for you to enter a new season. It doesn't have to be your marriage, but maybe it needs to be your expectations of marriage. Maybe it's your attitude toward your spouse or partner. Be willing to let some things die so new things can grow and take their place.

I didn't want to let go for such a long time. I didn't understand that death was necessary for something else to grow in its place. I had to let my anger die so I could have peace. I had to let my need to be heard and understood die so I could move forward. You can't convince people who are committed to misunderstanding you. You can never change the way they see you, never. This applies to every area of your life, not just marriage. Some people are seasonal—let them go. Let winter do its work in your life.

I have never given up something without something even better taking its place. It's never happened in all my years. Take the jump! Be bold and try something completely different. Your happiness is on the other side of your courage. Embrace the seasons changing in your life and learn how to find things to be grateful for. Gratitude will help you transition well into your next season. How you end one season is how you'll enter the next, so begin and end with gratitude.

Black/White

While having a conversation with my mother, I said, "Mom, there's no black and white here. It's going to be all shades of gray." There was so much truth and wisdom in that statement. I think all of us expect adulthood to go better than it does. We expect to know the answers to the hard stuff or at least have it be black or white. It's not. It's millions of shades of gray—we get to define it and redefine it repeatedly. You decide how to proceed. Feel empowered to believe and hope for something amazing, whether that's staying married or letting go.

I hope you stay married; genuinely, I do. I hope that man or woman decides and commits to fighting for you. They should wake up and realize they don't want to be apart from you. I hope they do the work to give you a love you are worthy of. That is sincerely my hope and prayer for your life. How that plays out will be unique, but don't discredit progress regardless of how small it seems. Stay grateful! Don't forget everything you've learned going through this. You are a new person and will be better for this. Hopefully, so will your spouse or significant other.

Don't feel pressured to define everything in your life right now. It's okay if your decisions look different from others. It's okay if you decide to try again a hundred more times with your marriage. In fact, I applaud and deeply respect your effort. Find significant ways in which you and your marriage can improve and do that good work. Don't give up and feel hopeless. It's worth every ounce you have left in you to try again. It's okay if you need to let it go and start again alone.

For the Mamas

The thought of divorce is more difficult when there are children involved. I know from daily experience that my heart breaks the most for my daughter. I would endure endless torture and pain if it meant she would be happy. As a mother, you are hard-wired to sacrifice everything for your babies. I look into my daughter's eyes and it damn near shatters my heart every day. She's amazing and deserved no part of what's happening. I hate it with a passion, but I also know it's a part of her story that will shape her.

I cannot call her to respect herself, love herself, and have high standards if I can't do that for myself. My greatest fear became having her see me as a hypocrite—having her see me suffer through my marriage, being constantly rejected, not fully loved, and screaming it in my face during her teenage years. That thought is so real for me! Instead, I want her to see the warrior in me who chose something hard, but ultimately led to the best future. I need her to know that in life sometimes you must do it scared.

For all the mamas who are reading this and wondering if they're making a good decision, I can't tell you that. What I can tell you is that little eyes are watching, and little ears are hearing. What you're doing and who you are becoming affects your children. Who do you want them to be? You need to model that behavior for them. I know mothering with a broken heart is absolutely the hardest thing to endure. I'm living it with you, but I want you to know you can do this! You can be the best mom regardless of the storm you're in. It's already in you to do this.

I know you're tired. I'm tired too. There are days when I wish I could hop on a plane, sit on a beach, and cry my heart out. I have plenty of days when I feel I'm failing her. I let stress and anxiety get the best out of me—we all do it. We are not perfect, but they're not asking for perfection. They want you—their mom. Your babies want YOU! You are everything they need, and your love is enough for them. Don't forget that in the middle of your pain! No matter how cruel this life is, we still must show up and be our best, not only for ourselves, but especially for our kids.

If you decide to stay married, I applaud you. I hope your family and friends support your decision. If you decide to walk away from your marriage, I applaud your decision. Both take tremendous amounts of courage. Be the parent you've always dreamed of being. Don't let this rob you of one second of happiness with your babies. Also, know that it's not your job to be both parents. I felt I had to overcompensate for her father. I don't need to do that! I need to be me, only me. Not mom and dad; I can never make up for what he lacks. We play two separate roles in her life. Remember that when they fall short. Have grace for yourself when you do.

Chapter Nine: Things to Think About

BURN THE SHIPS!

This is going to be different for everyone, but to move forward, leave some things behind and never look back. You might have to do the scariest thing you can think of. Jolt yourself into some sort of reality that your life is drastically different and it will never be the same.

It's time to identify those ships. What can't come with you into the next season or the next chapter of your life? This can be people, relationships, emotions, old mindsets, habits, etc. One thing is for sure, something's got to go.

Ready to exercise?

1. Make a list. What are the things that simply MUST GO? They are no longer serving you, so burn them.

2. What will you replace them with?

SCRIPTURE REFLECTION:

"See, I'm doing a NEW thing! Now it springs up, do you not perceive it? I am making a way in the wilderness and streams in the wasteland."

— Isaiah 43:19 (NIV)

"A ship in harbor is safe, but that is not what ships are built for..."

— John A. Shedd

CHAPTER 10

Half-Baked Love

MAN, WHAT A JOURNEY it's been! I've laughed, I've cried, and I've eaten a lot of chocolate chips cookies. Not very grateful for the extra twenty pounds, but whatever. I've reread these pages dozens of times and each time I've cried less. A lot of these words still hurt as bad as the day I wrote them, but ultimately, I'm proud of myself. I made it to the other side of this. I have nothing completely figured out, but I've made peace with that. I can only control myself and, for the first time, that sounds perfect! This journey of love and life is crazy. It's incredible how much it can teach you when you sit down and become the student.

I wrote this is all as my therapy with the intention that someday it would help someone else. I don't believe we live any part of our life separate from other people regarding helping one another. This entire process has sparked a passion in me to help other women (and men) work through infidelity, marriage, and divorce. I want to see other people thrive in situations that would previously defeat them. I'm humbled entirely by my journey and honored that I would get to share it with even one other person. Our lives and our choices create a ripple effect in the lives of others, and we should take that seriously.

Purpose in Pain

My mother has always quoted scripture about God's promises throughout my life. In the moments she quoted the Bible, I would often get angry at her because I felt her words were empty and thoughtless (sorry mom!). It wasn't until later that day or night when those words would echo in my heart. God would never waste a hurt! I've heard this one phrase so many times from my mother. It has been an anchor in my soul that God sees even this. Regardless of how bad it was, it would never be time or tears wasted. He would redeem it somehow in His time. I believe that with every fiber of my being.

Some of the best life outcomes can be born after a traumatic life event. It jolts you back in line with your purpose or destiny. You can let it drown you, but why? Why not find a purpose in your pain? Why not dig deep and figure out what can you do with it or find who can you help? I think it's very easy to become selfish when you're hurt. I also think it's human nature to want to pull away from other people. You'll need to fight like hell to remain selfless, but it's worth it. I think trauma reveals who you are at your core. I've seen plenty of people go through trauma who are complete assholes. I've also seen people who remain kind and still go out of their way for others. Pressure only reveals what's already inside of you. Write that down somewhere because it's 100% true.

Pain can always serve a greater purpose, always. If you research the greatest thinkers and writers, heck, even some athletes, it may surprise you to know their stories. Their stories start off sad, poor, homeless, orphan, abandoned, etc. etc. These people determined in their minds at a young age that their pain would serve a purpose, and it did. It set their course to happiness and success. Pain can truly be a gift to your life if you allow it to make you stronger—if you allow the process to change you.

You will be stronger when this pain passes and discover a version of yourself hidden inside you all along. If you find yourself in these incredibly hard places, know you are already strong enough to get through to the other side. God never allows us to experience more than we can bear, although I know sometimes it's feels worse. Let the pain serve you. Sit with it, learn from it, and heal.

I firmly believe that when you know better, you'll do better. Likewise, in that you don't know what you don't know. Marriage was like that for me. I settled in areas that I never should have. I married someone's potential and not who they were. I would be lying if I told you I'm ready to love someone again. I don't know when I'll be ready for that. Right now, I feel my time is best spent being a mother and learning everything possible from this. What I know is that I'm a fierce lover. I love with everything I have and I deserve exactly the same and so do you.

So how will I do better next time? Well, for starters, I need to grow more. I need to be at another level to attract like-minded people. When you don't do the work to grow, you'll keep attracting more of the same. I'm sure you've heard the saying "you attract what you are." It's the law of attraction and it's pretty spot on. I don't want to attract or be with someone I've already been with, just with a different face and name. I want to attract someone who brings out the best in me and isn't afraid to tell me I'm wrong. Someone who is equally passionate, driven, humble, honest, and loyal. I need to level up in my own life and sit at my table alone. You need to know what you bring to the table. If you don't, you will end up settling for less. You will make mistake after mistake because you don't even know who you are.

Trauma shifts a lot of things inside of you for the better and sometimes for the worse. Insecurity can really take on a life of its own during a divorce. I've spent a lot of time feeling ugly and worthless in my marriage and I refuse to feel that way again. I fight everything that's insecure in me daily. The fear that I will never truly be loved and known is a battle for me. After enduring so much rejection, I don't even want to think it can happen again. It will many times over. Not in the same package, but life is full of rejection, and I need to process how to heal from that. I don't have all the answers. I'm one soul on the face of this earth sharing my experience, hoping it will help you with yours.

When I find love again, it will be something magnificent! I truly believe that! I don't know when that will happen, and it's not a focus, but I want to set my belief system to expect the best. I won't ignore the red flags the next time, I won't date someone's potential, and I won't try to fix someone I never broke. I'm going to reel in my Messiah complex. LOL! It sounds funny saying it out loud, but it's true.

All jokes aside, you can't be half-loved by someone. Love doesn't work that way. It's all or nothing. Marriage is a full-on commitment to another human being to give them the absolute best of yourself, not your leftovers. Genuine relationships are about honor, loyalty, honesty, and growth. I lived through a half-baked version of love and suffered immensely because of it. It was far from fair and very cruel. I'm just like every other woman who wants to share their forever with someone they love and who loves them in return.

Honor This

I had to learn how to honor this place in my life. I did it kicking and screaming. God willing, I will never be here again, and that deserves a time of reflection to honor what has happened inside of me in the last three years. I went from wife to mother to ex-wife to single mom. That's a lot of transition in three years. It's been tremendous, but I've also grown so much. We forget to honor the horrible moments, but remember they change you for the better if you let them.

I want to honor rejection right now because it taught me that rejection sometimes is divine protection. It didn't allow for false hope or deep connection. Instead, it showed me reality and the many fractures in my marriage. Being rejected revealed deep wounds I still carried from my parent's divorce. It highlighted parts of my orphan spirit, that I wasn't enough for someone to stay. It's hard to admit that and I say it with tears in my eyes. Your pain won't heal until it's fully revealed, and sometimes it's on different levels. I believe the revealing is God's kindness to us. He's saying, "This right here? I want to heal that."

I want to honor loneliness because it showed me who my real friends are. It highlighted the people who showed up without being asked, who made plans with me, and who surprised me with coffee or gift cards. If I wasn't in that place, I could've missed letting my friends and family help me. I don't like to bother anyone or burden anyone, so it's hard to let people help. I want to figure it out myself, but I'm so thankful for the friends who didn't let me do it alone.

Despair, I honor you because you taught me how to fight for every breath. There were so many days I didn't want to live. My heart was so heavy and broken I thought, *surely today I die*. I learned how to fight for my life in despair. I learned to pray like I never have before and feel the weight lift off my chest. I learned to encourage myself and push myself to dream again. I wrote a book; I wrote this book because of my despair. This life is a gift! Every breath is a gift, and we sometimes take it for granted. We think the bad times will never end, but they do. Now is not forever, this really will pass. Despair will keep lying to you, so rise! You've already survived your worst days.

I want to honor God in this. I can't tell you how many times through this process I wish He could sit on my couch. I'm serious. I've needed Him more than ever before, and I love Him more than ever before. He's been more faithful than I could ever be, and He's wrapped me in His love when my soul was at its darkest. So, God, Thank YOU! Thank you for reminding me the love I long for I already have in You.

Stay off Social Media

Ha! That was a sharp turn in a different direction, but hey, I've got to keep you on your toes! Social media can be very depressing when you're going through all of this. Also, it's not reality. Social media is everyone's highlight reel and some people's venting place. Both are unnecessary in your life! Social media is a great distraction from doing the hard work you need right now. If you want some solid advice, take a break from your social media. It's for your own mental health, trust me.

I follow an account on Instagram called Authentic Love Magazine (@authenticlovemag) and I can't decide if I'm inspired or depressed! Lol! The pictures of couples in love are so beautiful, but is that really what I need to be feeding into my brain right now? NO! I need to be reading books, working out, and spend quality time with my daughter. I don't need to escape my life; I need to live it! Do yourself the best favor and get off your social media! Take a break without announcing it.

You're not ready for the universe to know your relationship status. I have changed nothing about my relationship status and if I do, it will be private. You don't need that person from seven years ago DMing you about your life. Everyone who needs to know probably already does. Anyone else is nosey and curious. It's none of their business, so don't feel you have to include everyone in your life choices.

There's one more reason to stay off social media, especially if you're getting a divorce. You may see things you don't want to see, like all your pictures being deleted off your spouse's account. BURN! That one stung a LOT! It felt like someone punched me in the stomach when I saw it. As if deleting pictures erases the person or erases our marriage. I thought it was petty and immature, and I was even more angry with myself that it bothered me. It bothered me, and it still does.

It bothers me because I wanted this to get better, but I couldn't continue to wait on a decision that was glaringly obvious. It hurts that someone can delete you from their lives as if you meant nothing. Again, hitting the rejection trigger! But it's all good! People who can delete you that quickly were never for you anyway. I will remind myself of that repeatedly—someone who is for you and loves you won't erase you.

Self -Love

If you spend your life learning to do this, it is time well spent! I used to think self- love meant I would be selfish. That couldn't be further from the truth. The definition of self-love is having regard for one's happiness or wellbeing. You have got to love yourself to move forward and live again! I say live because a lot has died, self-love being part of that. You must love yourself to watch what's going into your body, to have boundaries, to set goals, etc. Loving yourself is what enables you to love someone else well.

Self-love will open the right doors and close the wrong ones. You won't settle. You won't be afraid to call things as they are and evaluate if something doesn't seem right. It takes courage to love the broken places in you and see worth. It takes courage to be vulnerable with yourself and others. Start speaking positive affirmations over your life and watch how your life changes.

I've struggled with self-love for years. While outwardly it appeared that I had it together, loved myself, and was making it, the dialogue inside my head was completely different. I have extreme negative self-talk. I will literally talk myself out of my future if I could—I don't believe I can do things, I don't believe I'm smart enough, cool enough, brave enough, etc. I downright sabotage myself before an idea can even get off the ground. It's the worst thing about me!

Why do I do that to myself? Well, ultimately, it's something I believe about myself, but this is the last year that will happen. It's easy to doubt and talk yourself out of your potential. We are constantly telling ourselves stories about what's happening in our lives, and we see everything through the filter of our pain and insecurities. The story I kept telling myself about my parent's divorce, about my career choices, my choice of a spouse, etc., has reinforced this feeling of not being enough. Not anymore! I'm done with that!

I'm learning to love myself all over again from a different story. The story where no matter what, I win. Winning means coming out stronger on the other side. I'm expanding my capacity to be the best version of me and love people better. I remind myself that I will have hard days, but that doesn't take away from who I am and what

I can achieve. I'm forcing myself to do it scared, regardless of whatever I'm facing. I've allowed fear to prevent me from reaching my goals. I've allowed my negative self-talk to keep me complacent and agreeing that what I had was good enough, but is it, though?

Settling for status quo is not good enough! We only get one life to live, and we need to LIVE it! Try all the things and fail! Fail again and then succeed. Keep pushing and praying until something changes and amazing things happen. I'm sad that it took me so long to realize this, and I'm thankful. Being a mom finally made me see it. Life is short, and it goes by so quickly. Love yourself enough to chase that dream. Love yourself enough to start again if you need to. Learn how to see the value and beauty in yourself because when you do, the universe will open to you. You'll attract people into your life that will value and love you at the same level you love yourself.

Let them Fall Behind

Don't be afraid to let people go! I'm loyal to a fault and I want to include all my friends on my journey and have them in my life forever. Realistically, that can't happen. Some will fall behind and eventually fall away. It's ok! You won't have room for new people to enter your life if your space is cluttered with old friends, habits, etc. You need to make some room! I heard a sermon once that talked about old mindsets and the preacher kept saying and shouting, "Everything must go!" In a lot of ways, it's true! How can you move forward when you are desperately clinging to the past?

If you've decided to stay married for the long haul, or even for the next few months to see what happens, you must let things go. You must abandon your need to be right! Let go of your pride and humble yourself to start over. I don't think an affair is the end-all of a marriage. I think what's done after the affair can be. You need to purge your heart and mind and make room for a better way of life. Obviously, what I did wasn't working, so I changed it! Find people smarter than you who have a splendid marriage. Spend time with people who are intentional about their relationship.

Your inner circle will determine everything for you. If the people in your inner circle struggle with their marriage, your marriage will struggle. If your circle is winning in their marriages, your marriage can benefit. Surround yourself with good people who are winning in their marriage and life. You become like the people you spend the most time with, or, as it says in the Bible, bad company corrupts good morals. It's one hundred percent accurate. It's all good and dandy to decide you want to stay married, but I can promise you nothing will change until you do and your circle changes.

Stay Vulnerable

I find it fascinating how many people view being vulnerable as a negative thing. They equate vulnerability with weakness, but it's the opposite. It takes incredible strength to be open and stay open after people have hurt you. Human nature wants us to shut people out that hurt us and it makes us very reluctant to let others in again. Here's

Half-Baked Love

the thing—everybody didn't hurt you, one person did. Not everyone will abuse or manipulate you. Not everyone has ulterior motives. Most people are just like you, wanting to find people to have a genuine connection with.

You need to keep your heart open to new possibilities in life and when you refuse to be vulnerable, you can't receive them. It takes so much courage to be vulnerable after an affair. I will be the first one to tell you that. I don't want to be vulnerable, but the more I give myself the opportunity, the better I am for it. It's scary as hell to put yourself out there because we can't predict the outcome. If you need to have control, vulnerability will not work. You need to put yourself out there regardless of the outcome. I've shared my story with more and more people, and I'm not scared of their response anymore. I'm not ashamed of what's happened and what the eventual result is. We can't control how other people will feel about our story, but that doesn't mean you shouldn't tell it.

What do I mean by putting yourself out there? Try new things, get a new hobby, or make a few new friends. Open your heart and mind to new possibilities for your life. Be brave. You might get hurt again, but it's okay. You are not starting from scratch; this time, you're starting from experience. You already know better, so you will make better choices about who deserves a place in your life. Trust yourself and listen to your heart. Pay attention to the energy people carry and how you feel when you leave them. These are your indicators, so trust them. You don't have to make excuses for people. Not everyone will get a seat at your table. That's healthy!

Stay Present

It's very easy to go down Memory Lane and keep reliving your failures, but it accomplishes nothing. It's punishing behavior. You do it because your life is in a healthier state and some part of you doesn't feel you are worthy of it, so you punish yourself by reliving the past. STOP! Read that again! Stop punishing yourself over what happened. No amount of thinking about it will ever change things. It happened, but it's also over. Sure, you're dealing with the aftermath of it, but the injury was inflicted, and that part is over.

I think we all wish we could go back in time and choose better. There are so many things I would do different. Although reflection is great, regret is a wasted emotion. We can't change any part of our past. All we can do is learn from it. Stop regretting what happened, what you said, what you did, etc. Learn from it and move forward. Enjoy the here and now because tomorrow is promised to no one. Learn how to stay present in your life. Overthinking can be so detrimental to your growth. Put one foot in front of the other and go!

Being present is a gift, and it's something that needs to be cultivated in your life. We all have a to-do list that is a million pages long and keeps us busy with work, home life, and pursuing our dreams. You will miss so many moments because you're trying to stay on a schedule or accomplish your checklist. I took an entire weekend to reflect on that thought alone. How much am I missing because I refuse to slow down and stay present in today? How many moments are rushed because I view them as insignificant compared to what needs to be done?

We are all guilty of this! My nanny took a picture of my daughter on a walk where she bends over to smell the flowers. It's still one of the most precious pictures I have because it speaks to my soul. We have beauty all around us, but we don't stop to see it or enjoy it. That picture captured my full attention to what was happening inside me; I couldn't take the time to enjoy the simple pleasures of life. When did I lose my childlike wonder for creation, for life itself? I let all the hard and the pain make me feel like I had to keep plowing through life. Life is not meant to be endured. We are meant to flourish.

You can learn so much from a child. Nothing is complicated to them—life is just as it is. They have such curiosity and enthusiasm about everything, but if you're not careful, you can also find that to be a little annoying. That's how you know you're an adult—life suddenly becomes kind of dull. We forget to stop and smell flowers and appreciate the simple things. We forget to stay curious and be enthusiastic about new things and new people. Instead, we sit cross-armed, impatiently waiting for the next thing. Stay in the present! Appreciate the now because it will never come again.

Recently I've been feeling the need to make things physically beautiful. I've started buying myself flowers to display on the mantle. I'm not usually a flower person, so it surprised me that this simple thing brought me so much pleasure. I'm thinking about going to Home Depot and buying a big pot of flowers to put outside on the stairs. It's weird because I'm not typically that person, but it feels like a new me is coming out—one who wants to appreciate the beauty in this life, someone who wants to create something beautiful.

Make a Home Again

This is going to sound very odd, but my house doesn't feel like a home to me. It didn't in my marriage either. I remember growing up in a house that always felt like a home. Sure, it wasn't perfect, people argued, but love was the overall presence in the house. I've never felt that in my marriage. There was no familiarity or comfort in knowing this person was for you. That's what family is supposed to be about, isn't it?

I've thought about that frequently, and I've changed it. They say home is where the heart is, but I also think home is where your peace is. There was no peace in my home for years. Now that the turmoil has died down, I want to build a loving home with my daughter and our dog. I've started redecorating my room and other parts of the house. I want it to reflect more of my personality throughout. My room is my sanctuary, my cuddle-up-and-be-safe-and-warm place. I want to establish little traditions with my daughter, things that she can look forward to as she grows older.

My mother did a phenomenal job creating traditions for me. She is the reason I love Christmas and the Hallmark channel. There was always so much joy and music in our house. Music adds so much to an atmosphere and my mother always kept it a happy one. I look forward to building all of this with my daughter. No family is perfect; you must be intentional.

Now that I have the space to breathe and be me again, I'm looking forward to having my place to myself because sharing a house felt chaotic. We both functioned so differently and it felt more like a roommate situation. It's time to rebuild my space. It's time to put all the happy energy back into these four walls and make it a home. I need this to feel like it's where I belong because for so long it didn't. At the end of the day, we all want to belong and be loved.

Here's to the Future

I promise you, this is not supposed to be my life! Does that sound familiar? What if it is, though? What if everything that has happened has led me to exactly this place and moment where I feel brave, strong, and free? What if all things really work together for the good? There really is redemption in all of this. I believe there is. I didn't get what I thought I wanted the miracle to be. My marriage was not restored, and that's okay. It's sad, but it's okay. The future is still bright and I'm still excited about the endless possibilities.

I'm choosing faith over my fear every day! I'm choosing to love myself on my worst days and give myself credit for showing up! I'm leaning into grace for myself and others. The future is going to be what you make of it, and no one has time to waste being bitter. No one. There's still so much to live for! It's time to get your butt in gear and start. Whatever that looks like is up to you—no one gets to decide the next steps for you. While that may seem terrifying, it really is so freeing that you get to decide what's next.

So, what's next for me? Write more books, start a podcast, maybe a vlog. Show up every day for myself and my daughter. Be the absolute best mother I can be. Tackle the hard questions with grace for myself. Be patient with others. I've written ten dreams I'm going to make happen and manifest into fruition. I want my capacity to love to expand beyond my fear and pain. I want to stand on the other side of this and say it hurt like hell, but I am so much better for it. It's looking pain in the face and saying teach me, I'm here for it.

I get it that not everyone will say that or do that. I get it. It's excruciatingly difficult to keep that mentality when you're getting your butt handed to you, but stay in the game. Put your head down against the wind and keep going into it. The only way out is in. You must keep going no matter how hard it is. Giving up on yourself is not an option. The easiest way to do that is to stop dreaming and stop growing. You're going to have days when you're scared, but do it scared anyway. Muster up all your courage and try something new. Stop talking yourself out of your best life. You are ultimately responsible for where your life is going. Do something amazing with it.

What's the Takeaway?

There are so many things that I've learned from all of this. I could probably write a million books. Pain gave me an education in relationships and marriage that I will never forget. I learned more about relationships during this process than what my degree in psychology taught me. Seriously! Here are a few takeaways from my journey that I've learned:

1. Practice gratitude
2. Be humble—ask for help
3. Master self-care
4. Create safe spaces for yourself to heal
5. Pray/ meditate daily
6. Be a student of life

7. Live your best life NOW
8. Stay vulnerable
9. Growing is the WIN
10. You will overcome!

I know when you're in the middle of this chaos, the last thing you think is that you will overcome, but you will. It feels like you're being defeated, but you're not. You are going through an intense growing season. Please choose to grow through this and not go through this. You will be better for it! I hope you know how valuable you are to this world and the people around you. Don't let another person's behavior or mistakes make you feel less-than because they have nothing to do with you. It's stuff going on inside of them. Believe that. Don't blame yourself ever again for anything that happened. If you put in all the effort and do the work to make it better and it still doesn't work, be proud of yourself. You did your best!

You need to be proud of yourself and the person you've become in this process. I sincerely wish you all the beautiful things in life and that your summer season will come soon, but also learn to appreciate the winter. Every part of your life has to do with your perspective and how you train your mind to understand it. Most people don't do the work to train their thoughts and let them run crazy. You will drive yourself crazy if you can't get a hold of your thoughts. Your life moves in the direction of your thoughts. Remember that. You can be as miserable or as happy as you think you can be. It's time to move forward. There's no need to obsess over what's happened. You can't change it and it will no longer serve you to do so.

Half-Baked Love

I'm typing this out as my daughter lies next to me watching Despicable Me and I can't help but smile knowing that everything will be alright. I made the right choice even though it was a hard choice. There's peace in my heart, and that is priceless. There's still some sadness that rises now and then, but that's normal. It's all a part of healing. I've let go of so much to get here and I'm honestly so freaking proud of myself. I hope one day my daughter can see the strength it took to get here and be proud of me. She's the only thing that matters to me. My desire is for her to be healthy in all areas and that she becomes a kind, loving, and responsible adult. I want her to take risks and dare to dream big dreams. The sun is finally shining, life is coming back, and it will be beautiful! I'm so excited about what the future holds for me! I know one thing is for sure—I won't let fear keep me stuck ever again.

Ladies, life is seriously so beautiful. I know it's hard and unfair sometimes, but those moments get eclipsed when you think about how blessed you are to have family, friends, health, breath in your lungs, and peace in your heart. Stay grateful! Be humble and don't let pride keep you from growing up. Guarding yourself from further injury can cause you to become very prideful—don't do it. That pride will turn into bitterness quickly. Choose to remain humble, even if you're right.

This is random, but I want to apologize to myself. I'm sorry I didn't believe in you and trust you. I'm sorry that it took me so long to realize what you were capable of. I'm sorry that I let fear keep you from reaching for more and that I didn't know how to talk you out of being scared. Today is a new day, and this starts a brand-new life! I encourage you to apologize to yourself, too. Forgive yourself. You've done the best with what you had in your hands. You've done tremendous work to get to this point and you should be proud of yourself. You are worthy of every good thing, and you can have it if you choose to. I know it's crazy, but seriously, YOU'VE GOT THIS!

Chapter Ten: You Did It!

We made it through this book! Thank you from the bottom of my heart for taking the time to read my story. I've been terrified to put it all out there. But here I am practicing some major vulnerability. Fear is nothing compared to impact. I hope reading my story encourages you.

If my story resonated with you, changed you, inspired you, or you know someone who might need help, SHARE IT! Send me a DM on socials, tag me in a post, or gift it to a friend. We are not islands, and my favorite thing is reading a book recommended by a friend.

Do you feel ready and brave enough to conquer your mountain? I hope you do. I hope you've read my story and feel inspired to live your own in a much better way.

Your final mission:

BE HAPPY AGAIN!!!!!

Journal about how far you've come, and you'll find the glimmers of hope. Honor the process, and honor yourself, because even on your worst days, you've made it this far.

I'm proud of you. I'm proud of us. We've got this!!!!

"When you're brave enough to say goodbye, life will always reward you with a new hello."

— Paulo Coelho

Acknowledgements

God—Heavenly Father, I want to thank you first because I wouldn't be here without You. You carried me through the darkest and most painful season of my life. I never once doubted that You wouldn't come through for me and You did. You always will.

Ryan—God sent you to me. You have been a constant when my world was in chaos. You've taught me so much about life, love, and even writing. I'm so incredibly thankful for you and the peace and love you bring to my life. You've seen me cry more than anybody in my life and you've always been empathic and kind while adding the challenge to be better and push for more. You are a gift to me, I love you. I couldn't have finished without your support.

Mom—you're my biggest fan always! I consider myself extremely blessed to have the best mom in the world. No one loves quite like you, so fiercely and so unconditionally. Thank you for encouraging me to finish, for believing in me, and for all the shopping trips to find the outfits for the book cover and pictures. I love you, Mom!

My parents—Dad, Liz, and Carlos what a special group of characters we all are. I love you all and I wouldn't be the person I am without you. Thank you for your commitment to each other for learning and growing through navigating blended families. Your example showed me what's possible with starting again. Thank you for supporting me through all the seasons of my life and for being the best grandparents for Nava. We are both blessed!

Kaitlin—my personal photographer for life, but more than that, my dear friend. I'm so thankful our paths crossed years ago, and we've remained in contact. You are a phenomenal woman, friend, and photographer. Thank you for being on board with this project and for being my hype woman while shooting pics. I wouldn't have trusted anyone else to do this with me!

Ronei—Thank you! Thank you! Thank you, for being my editor and my friend. You encouraged me so many times during this process. I doubted myself so many times, but you were always there to remind me someone needed to hear this message. Thank you for believing in me and believing in this story. I'm forever grateful.

Acknowledgements

Tyler—my dear brother! You have made me laugh so hard to the point I'm crying. I love you so much! Thank you for getting excited with me about my book. Thank you for the long talks and dreaming big with me. It's been such a meaningful experience to share with you. I'm sending you a box of paper straws. LOL!

Vanessa—I'm thankful you're my older sister. We might not always get along, but I know for sure you will always be there. We've both overcome so much along the way and I'm so proud of you. I love you forever and I hope you actually read this book. I know you hate reading. The audiobook is coming just for you!

To my close friends, what can I say?! We've been through so much together and we are all still alive and kicking. Oksana, Melanie, Danika, Melody, Sumerr—you've seen it all and never judged me. You held my arms up during this nightmare and I can never repay your kindness, your love, and your encouragement. You kept reminding me I would be okay, and I am. Thank you will never be enough! We did it guys! We wrote and published a book!

To all my readers and people I've met along the way—Thank you for your support! Thank you for buying the book and sharing it with your friends and family. For allowing me to share my story in the hopes it would help you navigate yours better. I really can't put into words how much this book means to me. It's the first of many and I hope to take you all on the journey with me.

Finally, to the women who have shared this same pain and journey, I pray that God moves on your behalf. That you would be surprised by His incredible kindness and love for you. As you wait for the undefined miracle, I hope you choose growth. I hope you know that you are powerful and so worthy of love. Don't let anyone half-love you. You are enough! In fact, you are more than enough. You've got this!

About the Author

VERONICA COLÓN is a born-and-raised Jersey girl who moved to Nashville thirteen years ago. Nashville is one of her favorite places in the world and the place she calls home. She is a single mom raising a beautiful daughter who is her Mini-Me with all the personality and sass.

Veronica holds a degree in Psychology with a concentration in Life Coaching from Liberty University. She has a passion for helping other women overcome traumatic life events such as divorce and seeing them thrive again. Veronica is a bubbly, empathic, and passionate individual. She enjoys trying new local coffee shops, spending time with her daughter, all things summer, and dogs.

Connect with Me on Social Media

Instagram:
@missveronicacolon

Facebook:
https:www.facebook.com/
missveronicacolon

TikTok:
@missveronicacolon

Website:
www.missveronicacolon.com

www.ingramcontent.com/pod-product-compliance
Lightning Source LLC
Chambersburg PA
CBHW022015290426
44109CB00015B/1175